BREAKING THE BOUNDARIES

Yvonne Allen has a background in education and information services. Her activism began with opposition to the Vietnam War and the rise of the Women's Liberation Movement in the late 1960s and early 1970s. She was the first coordinator of Adelaide's Women's Studies Resource Centre in 1975, and was involved in the women's health movement. Now retired from the paid workforce, she works with the Kaurna people in her local community and is convenor of a small Adelaide-based NGO working in western Myanmar (Burma), India and Malaysia to improve health outcomes, particularly in relation to HIV/AIDS, and support education for refugee children.

Joy Noble has worked as a social worker and administrator in South Australia, and as a community worker with women in New Guinea. She was the first woman to be appointed, in the early 1970s, to the position of regional director in South Australia's Department for Community Welfare. Her books relating in particular to volunteering have sold widely throughout Australia. In 2002, she was awarded an AM for 'services to the development of the principles and practice of volunteering and as a contributor to the academic body of knowledge in the field of volunteering'.

Also by Joy Noble

Volunteer Management: A Resource Manual
(with Margaret Curtis)
Dear Chris: The challenge of working in the Community
Volunteering: A Current Perspective
Volunteers and Paid Workers:
A Collaborative Approach Volunteering SA
Australian Volunteers at Work: 101 Stories
(with Roger Dick)
Volunteering Visions
(with Fiona Johnston)
Imagine If: A Handbook for Activists
(with Fiona Verity)
Volunteer Program Management
(with Louise Rogers and Andy Fryar)
Positive Ageing: Think Volunteering
(with Louise Rogers)
Wow! The Wonders of our World
(with Fiona Johnston)

BREAKING THE BOUNDARIES

AUSTRALIAN ACTIVISTS TELL THEIR STORIES

Edited by Yvonne Allen and Joy Noble

Wakefield
Press

Wakefield Press
16 Rose Street
Mile End
South Australia 5031
www.wakefieldpress.com.au

First published 2016

Cover designed by Liz Nicholson, designBITE
Edited by Molly Jureidini, Wakefield Press
Text designed and typeset by Wakefield Press

National Library of Australia Cataloguing-in-Publication entry

Title:	Breaking the boundaries: Australian activists tell their stories / edited by Yvonne Allen and Joy Noble.
ISBN:	978 1 74305 418 5 (paperback).
Subjects:	Civil rights workers – Australia.
	Human rights workers – Australia.
	Social reformers – Australia.
	Social action.
	Social movements.
	Social participation.
	Voluntarism.
Other Creators/	Allen, Yvonne, 1942– , editor.
Contributors:	Noble, Joy, 1925– , editor.
Dewey Number:	323.0922

Contents

Introduction

What makes an activist? What makes one person speak out against injustice while another will be content to get angry at the TV news? What makes the activist so determined to make her or his voice heard, often against powerful odds or the gentle encouragement of friends and family to give it up as a lost cause? This book looks for answers in the personal stories of 46 Australians.

When Joy Noble and Fiona Verity wrote *Imagine if: A Handbook for Activists* (2006), they described a flexible 10-step plan for action that required thoughtfulness, courage and creativity, all underpinned by the values and beliefs of social justice, human rights and sustainability. The people who tell their stories in this book display, in different ways, these core qualities, values and beliefs.

What becomes clear as you read the stories is that activists come in many guises: teenagers, grandmothers, lawyers, children, parents, ex-politicians, workers, students, grandfathers. They can be the man next door or the woman in the shop you frequent. They can be a farmer or a newcomer to our shores. They are everywhere.

Their activism takes many forms:

- raising public awareness and focusing attention by speaking out;
- setting directions for new or improved policy, legislation and services;
- initiating or joining action groups, protests, boycotts and campaigns to bring about change;
- sending ideas, petitions or pleas to the media, people in authority and those who have influence on public opinion; and
- establishing ventures which build stronger communities.

Today we face dramatic changes in climate that are beginning to transform the globe as we have always known it. We see millions of people on the move displaced through famine, poverty and war. The near collapse of the global financial system in 2007–2008, which destabilised relatively prosperous national economies, has generated widespread hardship, anxiety and unease. Global terrorism has created an insecurity that has lead to intolerance and distrust, at times fuelled by governments intent on creating a culture of fear of the 'other'. We are reminded daily of the growing chasm between the 'haves' and 'have nots' in our Western democracies. Sometimes it seems as if it is all too hard, and nothing can be done.

The people who have contributed to this book, young and old, show us that this is not the case. Working across a range of areas, including human rights, the environment, ecological damage and resource depletion, gender issues, politics, disabilities, indigenous rights, food consumption, multiculturalism and the arts, they have broken the boundaries erected around them by governments, institutions, corporations, public opinion and sometimes themselves, and acted.

A book of this size cannot hope to do justice to activism in all its forms. There are major areas of achievement in which we fail to offer a voice, and we have concentrated our efforts largely in southern Australia. All we can hope is that our contributors have told their stories in a manner worthy of all those activists who continue to work toward making our world a better and fairer place.

We want to encourage people to do something when they see a need for change. The first step is often the hardest; but ordinary people can do extraordinary things, and working together we can make a difference.

Yvonne Allen and Joy Noble

Sierra Leone to Australia: The long road to action

KHADIJA GBLA

To understand how I became an activist you have to know my story, because my activism comes out of all the things that have happened to me. It has made me the person I am today.

I was born in Sierra Leone on the west coast of Africa in 1988. Until I was three, life was good. My grandfather was a chieftain with three wives and many children. Then the civil war broke out. We went to bed one day thinking life was safe and the next day there were bombs all over the place and people were killing each other. My mum told us we needed to hide, so they would not come for us. But finally, when I was ten, they did. That's when she put my baby sister on her back, took me by the hand and we ran. Along the way we saw things that no child should ever see. That was the end of me viewing the world in a fluffy pink dream.

We managed to escape and after a long journey we ended up in Gambia, trying to survive with thousands of other refugees.

It was there that our story began to change. You see, my mother had gone to teachers' college when she finished school. My grandfather decided that all of his daughters would have an education, which was unusual then. His decision saved our lives – it prepared my mother for what was to come. The unofficial refugee camp was a place where you went to bed with one eye open because you were waiting to be killed or raped. If you had no skills you did anything to survive: even selling your body or that of your daughters. But my mother could work as a teacher and support us. That's how I learned of the power of education. Diamonds and gold can run out, but having an education stays with you. Her education also made it easier for her to get refugee status. It took three years to be accepted by Australia. When people told us that Australia was at the end of the world, my mum would say, 'Here or there? Even if it is the end of the world, I choose there. I want to give my kids a better future. This is our only chance.'

We arrived in June 2001. We were the first Sierra Leoneans in South Australia. I was 13. It was winter, and cold. The streets seemed so empty. When we found an Asian grocery nearby, life became a bit more normal for us. We found African food – peanut butter and okra and, more importantly, chilli.

Starting school was hard. I had been transported into a culture very different from the one I knew. My mother enrolled me into a girls' school. I think she thought that girls would be less racist, or maybe she wanted to protect me from the young boys. I became the first African to enrol at Mitcham Girls High School. I was the guinea pig – it was a weird experience. The other girls seemed so innocent. They'd had a childhood. Not me.

I didn't feel confident to speak out, to get things wrong and be laughed at. I would come home crying. I didn't want to go back to school. This was hard for my mother. I remember she said, 'You escaped bullets and guns and bombs, and you are afraid of a bunch of little girls?' I wanted her to be more sympathetic to my plight, but it gave me a bit of confidence too and I started standing up for myself.

Then I started getting sick. When I first arrived from Gambia there was a lump on my neck that began swelling up. They said it was a rare form of TB. Doctors took the lump out and gave me medication. But I got worse instead of better. I was always exhausted and out of breath. I couldn't sleep. I had no appetite. I was having nightmares. I didn't want to talk. I didn't want to hang out. It felt to me like the Australian environment was bad for my system. By now I was in Year 9 and Year 10. No one could tell me what was wrong.

Me being sick represented Mum's lost hopes. She had brought me here for a better life and I was unable to benefit from it. By this time my little sister was in primary school and Mum was studying to be a registered nurse. She was working very hard on her studies, so it was me and my sister looking after ourselves most of the time. But I became so sick I couldn't even be a big sister properly. I had hit rock bottom. The doctors began talking about chronic fatigue and depression.

In Year 10, it was suggested I talk to a psychologist. My mother was against this. In our culture we do not have a sense of mental health; you are either crazy or possessed by the devil. Finally I said to her, 'We have tried everything. I might as well try this.' That was a good thing because the psychologist got involved in my schooling.

One day Mum sent me off to Women's Health Statewide to get my resumé fixed up, and I met René Weal who ran the Female Genital Mutilation (FGM) program there. That was when I began to think about what had been done to me, and it marked the beginning of my activism. I became a peer educator and provided a cultural perspective in the FGM workshops.

Soon after, I wandered into Multicultural Youth SA (MYSA) and met Carmen Garcia, who was to become my mentor. I was now in Year 11. She was interested in mental health among refugee communities and invited me to speak at workshops to give a youth perspective. I could speak about my own experiences. The more I did, the more I realised that I had a voice, had something to say.

MYSA provided a haven for me. By becoming involved I was beginning to work out my problems for myself. It was the therapy I needed. I saw that we Africans were having difficulty as a group, but the older generation didn't want to admit this, so the services provided didn't meet our real needs. Our elders were pretending, after the struggle to get here, that all was well and good. My mum was ashamed that I might have a mental health problem. She was afraid it would be on file and it would work against me in the future.

I was just a schoolgirl then, but I knew that if we didn't speak out about the real problems we were facing, we would get nowhere – especially us young people, some of whom were committing suicide. Now we were African–Australian. We had an identity crisis. I look back and think in 2003–2005 the refugee atmosphere was tough. Communities were working against each other, with lots of internal conflict. Nobody was representing us at a national or local level. We didn't have a voice.

Because of my work with MYSA, I was invited to speak at lots of consultations. Then I was selected to be on the SA Minister's Youth Council where I could represent the multicultural voice. I worked on mental health issues and, at the end of my time, got funding for MYSA to run the first multicultural youth mental health workshop.

In 2008, I was invited to attend the 2020 Youth Summit in Canberra. In an interview before I left, I raised the issues of mental health in refugee communities and female genital mutilation. My community was very upset. 'Why is she saying we are all crazy and stupid and retarded?' they said. I got angry phone calls and people complained to my mother. But as a result of the mental health report from that conference, there are now programs to help our young people to fare better in schools and deal with mental health issues.

I continued to talk about female genital mutilation and, in April 2013, was invited by Tanya Plibersek, federal Minister for Health, to attend the first FGM conference ever held in Australia. Before I knew it, I was speaking to a room full of politicians, doctors, nurses and other experts, and telling them my own experiences with FGM. It is a very difficult subject to talk about, but I discovered that with a bit of humour, I could break the ice. There was a big media response to my talk and I began to see just how powerful personal stories can be. Everyone wants their privacy, but some things are bigger than yourself.

When I found myself in an abusive relationship, I decided again to speak out publicly. Here I was, an SA Young Australian of the Year, and even I couldn't defend myself. I found a court-imposed restraining order didn't stop me from being stalked, and the police did not protect me. Once again, my community wanted me to remain silent, because otherwise I would get my abuser into trouble. Later my domestic violence support worker rang me to say I had done more for the domestic violence issue by speaking out as I did than they had been able to do in years. One day I want to have a daughter. How could I look her in the eye if I did not stand up for all women who are victims of domestic violence?

I sometimes think the wider Australian community is more proud of me than my own community, but that's true of many people who work for change. Activism, for me, is a journey that keeps changing form and shape. The things that we have to do to make the world a better place are obvious, but we have to choose to see them. Being an activist is about being more than just you. It is about creating a better world.

◇◇

KHADIJA GBLA *is now running her own cultural consultancy offering cross-cultural training, mentoring and motivational speaking. She is spearheading a campaign on change.org to end FGM in Australia and is planning a magazine for multicultural young women. She has received a number of awards for her work. In 2014 she was listed as one of the 50 most influential women in South Australia by the* Advertiser *newspaper.*

Social media in times of crisis

MEL IRONS

The Tasmanian bushfires of January 2013 were the state's worst in more than 40 years. Thousands of people were displaced, hundreds of homes were destroyed and thousands of hectares of bush and farmland were burnt. This is a story outlining the work I did in the immediate aftermath of the fires, and the work I continue to do.

On the afternoon the fires struck, I was stuck at home working and babysitting for a friend. Since 2006, I have been running my own business from home. At the time I was also working toward completing a PhD in Psychology. I live in an area that has been hit by bushfires before, but we weren't under any threat from these particular fires. I was listening to updates on local radio and monitoring the Tasmanian Fire Service website. Already stories were circulating about homes being destroyed, people being evacuated and others being trapped. Many of the details were murky, but it was clear a crisis was unfolding.

I had no experience of working in a fire situation, or anything to do with emergency management in general. I was anxious to help but was limited by my experience and immediate situation. I posted a few questions on Facebook and details started to emerge: there was a refuge centre that needed volunteers; people were worried about their pets; others were offering donations. This was only the beginning, but I had a strong sense that all this information – all this goodwill – needed to be organised. It was only a general thought, but it was enough to get me started on making the 'Tassie Fires – We Can Help' page.

I was not a social media expert (and I'm still not!) and I can't pinpoint why I acted on my desire to help. I had a thought, and I carried it out. I know I was emotionally connected to what was happening. It was clear at that stage that the worst of the fires were burning in the south-east, near the town of Dunalley. Friends of mine either lived in the area or had family there. This wasn't something happening in some far-off place on a map. In my mind I could see the eucalypts, the small country houses and the beaches. And from my house, I could see the smoke.

The fires in the south-east were on two peninsulas, which are connected to the rest of Tasmania via the same highway. When the road was cut off, thousands of people were stranded behind the fire front. Homes lost power and telecommunication services were completely down. Hundreds of tourists holidaying in the area were also stuck. There was a tremendous hunger for information – from those trapped behind the fire front, and from those trying to reach them.

I set up the Facebook page with the general idea that it could be something of a clearing house. People could post with requests or problems, and solutions would be found (I hoped). I called my local ABC radio station, which at that time was providing rolling coverage of the emergency. I explained what I'd done and encouraged people to get involved.

Within a few hours the page had attracted 16,000 'likes'. This number peaked at 20,815. People flocked to the page to get information, to ask questions, to give support and to see what was needed. There were updates from police and emergency services, information from various charities about what they were doing and how people could contribute, while thousands of volunteers shared information about what they were doing. I was on the laptop and phone for up to 20 hours a day, posting new content every three to four minutes. That became my job.

One of the stories which helps illustrate the page's role and impact concerns the plight of a particular oyster hatchery in Dunalley. The hatchery contained 60 million baby oysters. About 40–45 per cent of the oysters grown in Australia come from this business. It also employs 35 people locally. The hatchery only narrowly escaped the flames but in the days following the fire, another crisis emerged. Power had been lost and there was nothing to keep the oysters cool. Baby oysters are very sensitive to temperature, even slight changes cause stress and can eventually kill them. A distraught local farmer contacted me. He had already seen people using the website and figured it was his last chance to get some help. On 6 January (about 36 hours after the fire) I posted the following message on his behalf:

URGENT

ARE YOU AN ELECTRICIAN, AN ELECTRICAL ENGINEER
OR OWN A BIG, BIG GENERATOR?
Can you contact someone who is or does?
Dunalley needs you NOW ...

The message detailed the type of generator needed, as well as contact details for the hatchery and the emergency services people that would be needed to ensure people were able to access the area.

The following morning, I was able to post the following message from Ben, the owner of the hatchery:

READ THIS FOR SOME ABSOLUTELY AMAZING NEWS

Just speaking to Ben, the owner of Cameron's Oyster Farm. Yesterday I got on to them because they desperately needed some big generators, electricians, and electrical engineers. The word went out here and I rang the ABC too.

Here's what he had to say today:

We have managed to save an estimated 80% of our livestock at one of our sites - we are thrilled about this. 35 jobs in the local community have been SAVED. We have over 200 customers in other areas in Tassie and in South Australia who rely heavily on us to supply livestock - so we have literally saved dozens of families and family businesses in regional Tas and South Australia.

This is all because the word went out and we got generators and sparkies who came out and stayed out for there for hours yesterday.

So an enormous thank you to the Hobart community from Ben, the boss of Cameron's Oysters (third generation oyster farmer)

At present - they don't need anything 🙂

This one example showed how the page helped connect volunteers and provide immediate assistance. The owners of the hatchery are certain help would not have arrived in time if they had tried to go through the official channels. Throughout this crisis, there were hundreds of volunteers doing amazing things to help others. Some used the page, others probably didn't know it existed. But the ones that did use it found they could rely on it when needed.

My role as the administrator of the page was to channel, moderate and filter the information coming in. People were able to contact me directly either through the page or on the phone. I could post information on their behalf and they could also comment directly on existing posts. I liaised with local media outlets and emergency authorities as much as possible to ensure the information I was sharing was accurate.

In the week following the outbreak of the fires, more than 26,000 people were actively engaged with the page each day – meaning they clicked on a link, shared something or commented on a post. After 35 weeks, more than 2.6 million people were exposed to the page. Its role in the immediate aftermath of the bushfires became the subject of my new doctoral thesis, which I finished in August 2015. It looked at the way social media is used in times of crisis, as well as psychological first aid, community resilience and leadership. I have been asked many times to speak at conferences about why the page did what it did, why people used it in such a way. Now that I have completed my PhD on this topic, I have much more detailed answers, but these were my initial reflections about why the page was useful:

- Early successes (i.e. people getting help): built confidence among people using the page, and fostered the idea that it was a viable option. People were empowered and it helped keep the tone of the page positive.
- Fast: problems were solved, help was received ... quickly
- Accurate: the information posted on the page came from good sources, often from people who were 'on the ground' and knew what was happening. This included official sources (e.g. police, fire service)
- Accessibility: using the reach of Facebook, and I was there as the administrator for hours every day, available to respond to all requests
- Interaction: people could add their own information and insights to the page; it was a conversation, not a one-way broadcast, and I was responding to all posts.

There were other factors, but this provides some insight into how the page worked. Authorities often regard the social media space with suspicion, and emergency services as something that can't be trusted, and to be kept at arm's length. There's a view that it's too prone to rumour mongering or the spread of false information. These fears have some merit, but are usually blown completely out of proportion. They shouldn't obscure the fact that social media can also be tremendously beneficial during times of crisis, for example myth busting. In fluid, ever-changing environments, where information needs to be shared quickly, social media is a valuable communication tool. In fact, it's essential.

Personally, I get a bit tired of all the risk paralysis and fear in our community – the stuff that prevents good people from doing good things. I wasn't trying to be a hero or do anything extraordinary – I just wanted to help and I started helping. I negotiated, communicated, learnt, made decisions and learnt some more. I had no idea where it would all lead and I'm still finding my way. But the risks I took were worth it – for me and many others.

◇◇

MELANIE IRONS *has now completed her Psychology PhD on the way social media can be used in times of crisis. In addition, she runs a Tasmanian-based, award-winning personal training and health coaching business, Booty.*

The reluctant activist

JULIAN BURNSIDE

I probably have very little to tell activists, since I do not believe I am one. But people insist that I am one. If that is true, I am an accidental activist.

In my time as an activist, I have learned two main things: do what *you* are able to do, and never lose heart.

Some activists favour direct action; that is not something I know about. But I know about advocacy. Arguably it is the only thing I know how to do. So my 'activism' has mostly taken the form of speaking out against the things that trouble me.

When I started speaking out against Australia's mistreatment of asylum seekers, my purpose was to persuade the Australian public that what we were doing was cruel, immoral, pointless and grossly expensive. I told stories about the reality of seeking asylum. One story – a story that still haunts me – concerned an Iranian family: mother, father and two girls, aged seven and 11. They had fled religious persecution and managed to get to Australia. They were put in the Woomera Detention Centre. The condition of each of them gradually deteriorated, but the 11-year-old was in a really bad way. A psychiatrist visited Woomera to speak to the family. He wrote a horrific report in which, among other things, he said of the 11-year-old:

> She refuses to engage in self-care activities such as brushing her teeth. She has problems with sleeping; tosses and turns at night; grinds her teeth; suffers from nightmares. She has been scratching herself constantly. She doesn't eat her breakfast and other meals and throws her food in the bin. She is preoccupied constantly with death, saying 'Do not bury me here in the camp. Bury me back in Iran with grandmother and grandfather'.

She carried a cloth doll, the face of which she had coloured in blue pencil. When asked in the interview if she'd like to draw a picture, she drew a picture of a bird in a cage with tears falling and a padlock on the door. She said she was the bird.

After a number of pages to similar effect, the psychiatrist noted:

> It is my professional opinion that to delay action on this matter will only result in further harm to this child and her family. The trauma and personal suffering already endured by them has been beyond the capacity of any human being.

The report urged that the family be transferred to a metropolitan detention centre where the 11-year-old could get daily clinical help. Nothing happened. A month later the psychiatrist wrote another report, trenchantly criticising the detention centre management and the Department of Immigration for keeping the family in the desert instead of somewhere where they could get appropriate help for the 11-year-old.

Eventually the Department relented, and the family was moved to Maribyrnong Detention Centre, in the western suburbs of Melbourne. Although the reason for moving them was to make it possible for the 11-year-old to get daily clinical help, for the first two weeks of their stay in Maribyrnong, no one came to see her.

And on a Sunday night in May 2002, when her mother

and father and sister were in the mess hall eating dinner, the 11-year-old took a bedsheet and hanged herself. She did not know how to tie the knot properly, so she was still choking when the family got back from dinner.

She and her mother were taken to the emergency ward of a nearby hospital where she was put into intensive care. The lawyer who had been looking after their refugee application heard about this and went to the hospital at about 8.30 or 9 that night. He said hello to the detention centre guards, who were there so that mother and child were still legally in immigration detention. The lawyer didn't need to introduce himself because he is well known at the detention centre. He asked to see them and was told: 'No, you may not, because lawyers' visiting hours in immigration detention are nine to five.'

He rang me at home that night, and told me what had happened.

That case angered me then, and it angers me still. It made me determined not to rest until such obscenities could no longer occur in Australia.

But things got worse, leaving to one side the countless minor indignities that are the commonplace of any bureaucracy.

I spent the first week of November 2002 in Perth doing an inquest into the deaths of two women drowned when the *Sumber Lestari* caught fire and sank in the waters off Ashmore Island. It was carrying 162 refugees. One of the women who drowned, Fatima, was 20 years old. She had no surname. She was married to a man called Sayyed Husseini. From the day of the drowning, Sayyed was held in detention on Christmas Island.

After agitation from refugee groups in Perth, the Department agreed to bring Sayyed across to Fremantle so that he could attend the inquest into the deaths. A small concession you might think, but hard won. I was briefed to act for the members of the family. The matter went on for the whole week, and the last day of the inquest was Friday 8 November, which just happened to be the twelve-month anniversary of Fatima's death.

Sayyed had sat patiently in the dock – note that, in the *dock* – of the Fremantle Court. He had sat patiently there for the whole week listening to evidence given about the death of his young wife. He had given evidence at the request of the Commonwealth about the circumstances of the incident. It was a harrowing and traumatic experience for him, reliving the memories of the day on which the leaky craft caught fire and sank.

To mark the 12-month anniversary of the drowning, a support group had organised a small memorial service to be held in the park immediately adjacent to the Fremantle Court. The support group got permission from the Court, they got permission from the detention centre management, they got permission from the police, they got permission from the Department, that Sayyed should be allowed to step out of his cell and into the park just metres away, under guard, and attend the memorial ceremony for the death of his wife. Fifteen minutes before the ceremony was due to begin, Mr Ruddock, the Minister for Immigration at the time, withdrew permission for him to attend. Ruddock's excuse, apparently, was a concern that Sayyed might be photographed, and that that could cause trouble for him in Afghanistan.

The difficulty with that excuse was that the Department had already rejected Sayyed's claim for refugee status, which raised a question about what sort of trouble he might expect in Afghanistan merely for being photographed at a memorial service for his dead wife. He was deeply hurt by Ruddock's decision.

At the end of the evidence, when the inquest was winding

up, the coroner asked him if he would like to say anything. It is a courtesy usually extended to bereaved relatives. Sayyed spoke, quietly and with dignity. He finished by saying that he was grateful to the people of Australia for being kind to him during the inquest and he hoped that his evidence hadn't upset anyone. Such dignity and grace, after such a contemptible piece of cruelty, said a great deal about him; but it also said a great deal about Australia.

I have never thought anger a very useful emotion. But that day I felt anger which will never fully subside, and which wells up every time I see a Minister for the Crown acting contemptibly. Sadly, it happens a lot.

The Coalition, in government and in opposition, has relentlessly tagged boat people as 'illegals', which is simply false. Scott Morrison, the Minister for Immigration during the first 18 months of the Abbott government, took to urging that boat people who were to be placed in the community should be required to report to the police; that they should not be housed near 'vulnerable people' or near children. All of this rhetoric was calculated to create the false impression that boat people were criminals, that they were dangerous, that they represented a threat. When the Coalition won government in September 2013, Morrison took charge of the Department of Immigration and Citizenship. He renamed it the Department of Immigration and Border Protection. The unspoken message was, 'You need to be protected from these people, and we are protecting you'.

It is a great curiosity that Morrison, who claims to be a practising Christian, was willing to lie about a harmless group of people, and win electoral popularity by conspicuously mistreating them. With his lying and hypocrisy, Morrison made Ruddock look positively virtuous.

The 2013 election campaign was the first in Australia's political history in which the two major parties tried to outdo each other in their promises to be cruel to a group of human beings.

Australia's mistreatment of refugees demeans all of us. Arundhati Roy once said, 'The trouble is that once you see it, you can't unsee it. And once you've seen it, keeping quiet, saying nothing, becomes as political an act as speaking out. There's no innocence. Either way, you're accountable.'

I will keep speaking out for as long as Australia keeps betraying its own inherent decency. If that makes me an activist, I am proud to be one.

◇◇

JULIAN BURNSIDE AO QC *is an Australian barrister, human rights and refugee advocate, and author. He practises principally in commercial litigation, trade practices and administrative law. He was awarded the 2014 Sydney Peace Prize: 'For his brave and principled advocacy for human rights and for those wronged by government, for insisting that we respect our international legal obligations toward those seeking asylum, and for his unflinching defence of the rule of law as a means to achieve a more peaceful and just society.'*

Flying our Aboriginal flag

PHOEBE AND SAVANNAH BRICE

We live in South Australia in a small, close-knit community about 200 kilometres north of Adelaide.

Phoebe

Our story started in 2007 when our Mum explained to us what being Aboriginal meant. She told us we were different from other people. When we asked how, she said, 'It's simply because our skin colour is different and we have a different flag. When you're older you will understand better.'

We went to school the next day and when I noticed that our flag wasn't flying proudly next to the Australian flag I started asking questions. I asked my classroom teacher why and she decided to follow it up. She spoke with our principal and they both decided I should contact Mr Rowan Ramsey, our federal Member of Parliament, and ask for an Aboriginal flag. I was successful and also received a medal for my achievement and initiative. Sadly, the flag was never flown because we didn't have a flagpole to fly it on, and later, mysteriously, the flag disappeared.

After a few years, in 2012, my sister Savannah and I wanted to review this problem. We discussed it with our new principal, Maceij Jankowski, and our new classroom teacher, Katie Deverall, and decided that we would again write to Mr Ramsey asking for a new Aboriginal flag and an Australian flag too, as the old one had been put through quite a bit. But to prevent the dilemma we were earlier faced with, Savannah wrote to Mr Ramsey also asking for a flagpole.

About two weeks later we received a letter in the mail each and a parcel containing an Australian and Aboriginal flag. We had successfully gained two new flags for our school. But there was still the problem of the flagpole.

Savannah

Phoebe was lucky. Her letter came with a parcel of two flags. My letter was a disappointment. It said that the flagpole fund had ceased but the good news was that my request had been forwarded onto Mr Geoff Brock, our state MP, to see whether he could be of assistance.

I waited for around two months to get a reply from Geoff, and when I finally got one it said that he was trying and he had sent my letter on to other people.

Then it was the September school holidays and my family and I went to the Port Pirie Smelters Picnic. As we were walking along Sideshow Alley my mum spotted Geoff Brock and she told Phoebe and me to go over and talk to him. So we did. We shook his hand and told him about the school and the flagpole. He told us that he was planning to visit our school in the last term. When school started again, I told my teacher and the principal and they were very excited.

It was Monday of the last week of term for the year and Geoff Brock still hadn't come to visit, so I asked my teacher and principal for permission to send an email telling him how upset I was that he hadn't come. The next day the principal asked for me in his office. I thought I was in trouble but it turned out that Geoff Brock was going to be at my school at 10 am that day. When he arrived, the principal, Geoff and I had a short meeting updating me on what was happening.

Then it was 2013. Phoebe had started at high school. We didn't hear from Geoff until early in term two, when the principal called me into his office. He said that we had finally got the pole. I was so happy I started crying. A few weeks later the pole arrived and by that time some of the local reporters heard about the story and by the eighth week of term two, I had already been in six newspapers. In the last week of school we had a NAIDOC celebration where one of the other Rocky River schools came to celebrate with us. We had a huge flagpole ceremony. All the parents came, and both Geoff Brock and Rowan Ramsey were there along with news reporters. After Rowan and Geoff read their speeches, the school captain and I raised both the Australian and Aboriginal flags. For the first time in all my life at that school I saw my flag rise.

I would like to thank all of the people who were involved with getting the flags and pole, and all of my friends for their support, my teacher and my principal and, most importantly, my mum, dad, sisters Phoebe and Samantha, and my older brother Mathew.

At primary school it's a tradition that the Year 7s leave their mark. As I go into my last year here, I feel my mark has already been made.

◇◇

PHOEBE BRICE *plans on staying in school to finish Year 12 and continue on to university to become a paediatrician as she loves to work with kids, loves to help people and most of all loves bandaids!*

She will definitely continue to promote Aboriginal rights as it's a cause that is dear to her heart and her entire family's heart.

◇◇

SAVANNAH BRICE *has now joined her sister at high school and wants to finish Year 12, then go to culinary school to fulfil her dream of being a chef. Her passion is to make people aware of the traditional owners of this land and to educate people about equality.*

Outward action arising from inward stillness

ADRIAN GLAMORGAN

I say it began with hair length, but that's because I felt I could choose to resist. The truth is, I became a pacifist just before turning eight. Before then I'd been a rabid imperialist, growing up in Wales in the late 1950s and early 1960s, fighting Zulus at Rorke's Drift and, of course, defying Nazis in our imagined Spitfires. I revelled in the energy, belonging, and glorious fun of battle. But embedded, too, was a shared sense of justice, of good fighting evil: we boys played Robin Hood hiding away in forests from the wicked Sheriff of Nottingham, and the courage of D-Day. As a five-year-old I had seen on television the gassed Jews being thrown into the pits. The Nazis had to be fought. These doings made sense. Less so when I found war medals someone had inexplicably tossed away into building rubble.

My firm worldview about 'the other' was questioned to the core in 1965 when my family arrived in Sydney to start a new life, free of the greyness of class, hard weather, bad housing and village gossip. We moved into a flat in Randwick, on Alison Road. For the first time in my life I smelt onions frying on the stove from the Greek landlords in the house behind. They grew vegetables instead of buying them from the shop. It was all unfamiliar. And downstairs lived the first Aboriginals I saw, a woman with her child. Their dark skin was a mystery to me. I watched and gaped. They seemed gone in no time. And in their place moved several Colombo Plan students, studying at the University of New South Wales. A Muslim student from Pakistan, studying nuclear science, who prayed often, and did not care for my drawings of Mickey Mouse, scoffed when I said the British Empire was a good thing. I was puzzled, and had no ready answer, but he was kind and patient with me.

Then Eddie from the Philippines asked me to explain my game of Cowboys and Indians. Weren't Indians with their bows and arrows defending their land? Weren't the cowboys the ones trying to take it? My life turned upside down. Suddenly I could not bring myself to shoot Indians. From that day on I could not carry a toy gun. I heard the word 'pacifist', and knew I was one. The phrase 'citizen of the world' came to me, and I knew where I belonged.

A few months later at the family union day picnic at Cronulla, Father Christmas gave out presents to all the boys and girls. The best I knew, as an eight-year-old, was that Father Christmas knew every one of us, and judged us omnisciently. Not quite God or Jesus, but somehow related.

So at the union picnic I opened my present from Santa. A cap gun from the Wild West. For killing Indians. This made no sense. I looked around. All the boys were getting cap guns. The girls were unwrapping watercolour sets. I would have loved a watercolour set. Father Christmas would have known that. As he should have known I was a pacifist. So why this? Confused, I burst into tears.

So a seed grows. In the 1970s I grew my hair, because we were really saying 'Stop the war'. The war in question (for there are always too many wars) was in Vietnam. Old men in suits in federal parliament were sending boys only a little older than me as conscripts and volunteers to the jungles of Nui Dat. It seemed to me as a 13-year-old that Australia was messed up in politics we barely understood, in a place Australians couldn't find on a map, with an ally using cluster bombs, Agent Orange and napalm, burning villages like My Lai.

We moved to the Riverina of New South Wales. Growing long hair was bound to get me into trouble. 'You're a lovely girl,' taunted one elderly woman on the street, affronted by my challenge to masculinity. Being a teenage boy, still unsteady, her words cut me deeply. But I kept my hair long, because I was against the war. If the war was still going, I was ready to be a conscientious objector. I knew that, even as a 14-year-old.

My father didn't like the war in Vietnam. I doubt that he would have wanted me balloted into the madness of South Vietnam. All the same, he hated my hair long. My mother urged me to get a proper cut, to placate him. Amid domestic strife, I conceded. As I climbed into the barber's old iron chair in Albury, the barber snorted, and wound the cotton sheet tightly around my neck. 'Right,' he said, 'I'll fix you.' He gave me the worst haircut imaginable. When I got home my mother was horrified. She hadn't meant a basin cut like that. My father looked away.

Against wars, I learned to turn my other cheek. One day after a sports day, I had to catch our country railmotor from a small platform siding. As I approached, with a 20-minute wait ahead, a swarm of boys suddenly surrounded me. They pushed the younger one among them, a new kid, into my face. Everyone shouted, 'Fight! Fight!'

I would not fight this boy. I didn't really know who he was. The other boys had elbowed him into this for days. There seemed no escape from the flashing eyes and angry calls. With a twinge, I recognised there were no adults around.

'Fight! Fight!' But I would not. I would not fight, nor fuel their mob frenzy. I had heard Jesus' story about turning the other cheek. The boy sized me up. He punched me in the face. I felt the clap and sting, but didn't move. He hit me again. No movement. My cheek stang again, louder, more burn. He punched me again. Then more. My cheek was reddening, and sore. Again and again, the punches came. But I did not move. I would not fight. Eventually there was the shimmer of the rails as the train came up the line. The mad circle opened. We got on the railmotor. My cheek had swollen into a lump. An hour later I was home, blurting out what happened to my parents. 'Why didn't you fight back?' asked my father. Stammering, I walked away. No one understood.

The next morning on the way to school the boys asked me how my cheek was. My face was still swollen, but I reached for my *other* cheek in nonchalant defiance. That afternoon they tried a rematch. I was weary already. When he swung, I grabbed his arm and held him down. He was weaker than I could have imagined. I didn't hurt him, just constrained him. He didn't bother me after that.

A few months later I cheered as the tired old men in parliament were thrown out. In stepped the new lot with fresh ideas: conscription ended, weary soldiers came back, progress in all directions, and Australia prepared to become a new kind of country, even blinking with possibility that it would step outside the American military alliance and join peaceful, non-aligned nations. But then the king hit: in 1975 Gough Whitlam and his government were dismissed by the governor-general. I joined the first anniversary protest rally outside Canberra's old parliament. Eventually Gough Whitlam strode out of the white building and walked among us. We cheered, but he kept walking about, saying nothing, refusing to make a speech. Nothing. Our expectant cheers died down. Finally within a few paces of me, a Greek migrant blurted out: 'We've maintained our rage, Gough – where's yours?' The towering man stopped, blinked for a moment, smiled inconclusively, and I watched him walk on. The question lingers.

To survive as an activist, my anger about Australian indifference to atrocity, genocide and violence has had to transform. To survive, I aim to be the change I'm wanting to see. Quakerism – with testimonies of peace, community, equality, simplicity, integrity, and earthcare – has long supported my journey.

So where does activism start? 'How do you choose what to do, when there is so much that needs to be done?' as a friend once asked. There is no single answer: only *your* answer. Sometimes it might be growing your hair long; sometimes shaving it off entirely. It might be refusing the bullying mob, or sharing a way through. In a suffering world there are plenty of outer calls. My own best discernment comes with inward listening. There's an invitation waiting, offering to act out of deep transforming peace, needing no certainty of outcomes.

From experience, the inner answer connects. Through inner stillness, it's easier to take Rumi's journey, the one beyond the field of right and wrong. For when the complexities of evil assemble, I have found refuge in the transforming power of love, and the hope and trust that goodness is found in everyone.

ADRIAN GLAMORGAN *is a long-time peace, justice and environmental campaigner, with skills as a writer, facilitator, nonviolence trainer and educator. Along with Elizabeth PO' he produces, the weekly environment radio program 'Understorey'. Their series 'Beyond Nuclear War and Radioactive Peace', about Australian uranium fuelling Fukushima, and the lack of proper global governance of nuclear materials, led to both being recognised by the WA Conservation Council as 2014 'Environmental Journalists of the Year'.*

Pulping the mill

ANNE LAYTON-BENNETT

In March 2011, Tasmania was eight years into the campaign to stop 'the world's fourth largest pulp mill' being built in the Tamar Valley, and I was feeling increasingly panicked by my breezily given agreement a week or so earlier to speak at a Pulp the Mill rally. This was no longer to be a comparatively intimate action of around a hundred 'uniting on site'. Word had got out, so plans had been hastily revised in order to safely accommodate the anticipated thousand people, and Batman Bridge Reserve was now the venue. But while the threat of arrest for trespass had been removed, my public speaking debut would be before a considerably larger audience and, therefore, a lot more daunting.

So how did it come to this?

Before the well-documented fateful Hobart waterside lunch in 2003, where the pulp mill project was reportedly first discussed by former state premier Paul Lennon and Gunns' former chairman and chief executive officer John Gay, I was happily minding my own business and enjoying a satisfying if unremarkable life.

A photocopied flyer inviting The Householder to a community meeting provided the first hint something untoward might be afoot. I no longer recall whether the words 'pulp mill' were mentioned specifically, but I had lived in Tasmania long enough to know it was wise to activate mental alarm bells for anything that involved the name Gunns. Indeed such was its reputation, merely saying the name of Tasmania's largest timber company was enough for ears and noses to start twitching.

I first came to Tasmania as a tourist in 1979. Like others before and since I was enthralled by the island's multi-faceted and dramatic physical beauty, so different to that of Western Australia where I then lived. Its remote, wild and dramatic elements were reminiscent of parts of my native Yorkshire, and prompted the throwaway comment I made during that Tasmanian fly-drive holiday: a wish to one day live there.

Needless to say, I was less enthusiastic when the universe finally tuned in to this casual remark, having by that time happily transplanted myself into Perth's laid-back coastal lifestyle. Decision time arrived when my Tasmanian-born partner announced his long-held wish to return to his home state, a decision about which I was more than a little ambivalent.

Tasmania was in the middle of its third major environmental battle when I arrived in 1988; one that also involved a pulp mill, at Wesley Vale in the state's north-west. I remained a bystander throughout this campaign, being too busy adjusting to a different life as a small business owner and employer in my new home state.

When I first experienced Tasmania as a tourist, any disturbing environmental tensions had largely gone unnoticed. In hindsight I realise they must have been there all along, festering behind summer-time masks of friendly, welcoming hospitality. But by the late 1980s, these masks had splintered, exposing tensions each time the subject of forests, trees or pulp mills was raised.

Until that flyer in the letterbox – a piece of paper that certainly changed my life – I had managed to remain largely detached from this forestry debate. The catalyst was discovering at that fateful meeting in Deviot's packed community hall that plans for a pulp mill were once again being discussed, this time in the Tamar Valley. This location had been universally rejected in the 1980s due to the significant and insurmountable health risks pulp mill emissions would inevitably pose. The level of suspicion in the room was high due to the combination of secrecy, the knowledge its proponents were a company feared and mistrusted for the methods it employed to silence critics, and a state government whose close association with the forestry industry was being increasingly condemned.

My activist journey began with small steps.

The first involved dipping my pen into the political waters and writing a letter to the local newspaper about log trucks, and their noticeable increase on our roads. And a pulp mill had yet to be built. In the years since, I've written countless letters and emails to newspaper editors and politicians, and contributed numerous online blog comments.

However, stopping the pulp mill was always going to need more than letters to editors, so writing submissions was the next addition to my activist CV.

There were about 60 like-minded souls at the first submission-writing workshop. As partners in our collective concern we squashed ourselves good-naturedly into the tiny Launceston venue that had been made available. Many faces were familiar from the first successful mill protests, and there was soon a cosy informality about the evening among people from all walks of life (whose paths would normally not cross) because friendships were already forming.

I'd like to say my first matchless and meticulously referenced submission made a difference. But it, and the other 760-plus submissions received by Tasmania's Resource Planning and Development Commission (RPDC), were rendered null when Gunns withdrew from the process. However, the principal benefit of that crowded workshop was the ability and confidence to write all the other submissions necessary in the years since. Not all of them involved the pulp mill.

During the last 10 years a number of community groups have formed to fight the mill. The Tamar Residents Action Committee (TRAC) was the first. It emerged from the turbulent and anxious early campaign period, born out of those initial community hall meetings. It brought together people of all ages, backgrounds and social demographics, many of them veterans of Tasmania's previous environmental battles. But TRAC soon imploded, a victim of its leader's hubris and political aspirations. Its purpose had been served, however, because by now those of us committed to stopping the mill had all met, knew we could rely on and support each other, and had already gained confidence after organising several successful rallies.

So when Tasmanians Against the Pulp Mill* (TAP) formed from the ashes of TRAC, the transition was almost seamless, and membership assured. But with so many issues of concern associated with the mill – public health risks from toxic emissions, pollution risks to air and water, economic risks to existing tourism and agricultural businesses, and environmental risks to vulnerable marine and wildlife – other groups also formed, each with a different focus.

Pulp the Mill (PtM) began as a direct action group and was an offshoot of TAP. Its founder was one of three landowners who had unsuccessfully challenged the controversial *Pulp Mill*

---

* Since rebadged as TAP Into A Better Tasmania

Assessment Act 2007 (PMAA), with its widely criticised Section 11 clause that denies the right of any individual or business to claim redress should the mill impact negatively, in any way, on their health, wellbeing or livelihood. The fast-tracked PMAA was introduced by the state government after Gunns withdrew from the Resource Planning and Development Commission knowing the pulp mill was to be deemed 'critically non-compliant'. PtM initially focused on training people for 'peaceful community protest' during organised actions, and only branched out to include corporate campaigning as the overall campaign developed.

Other groups opposed to the pulp mill formed such as Friends of the Tamar Valley and Women Against the Mill (WAM!), and I'm far from being the only person to claim membership of them all. All groups are autonomous but work together when necessary for the larger rallies, forums and events. That said, some of the more creative, cheeky and powerful actions organised by WAM! have involved just four or five women.

Like many others I never imagined the campaign to stop the pulp mill would last 10 years, and counting. Nor did I imagine the extent of my involvement would be so great, or so personally challenging. Letters to editors are one thing; facing arrest, fronting national media, stripping naked on a freezing winter's morning along with 14 other women and, most recently, standing as a candidate for the Tasmanian Greens in the 2014 state election, are quite another.

If a policeman's hand on my shoulder and a day in court have still to be experienced, it's only because writing Pulp the Mill's post-event media releases from the back of a paddy wagon was deemed neither practical nor possible.

Throughout the campaign words have been my principal

weapon of choice. For 10 years the words flowing from the pens and keyboards of myself and thousands of others has helped hold potential investors at bay. Until that day in March 2011 my words allowed me to remain hidden behind my name, a name that is now closely associated with pulp mill opposition – the name that has been behind thousands of emails to hundreds of mill opponents.

The campaign to stop the pulp mill has been long and hard, and is still ongoing in late 2015, with continued uncertainty Gunns' receivers have found a buyer for the pulp mill (as numerous media statements have implied) and the mill permits, which remain valid until 2017.

The campaign certainly catapulted me out of my comfort zone. But there have been positives. Because of the campaign I've met some amazing and inspiring people I now count as friends. Like me, all are committed to ensuring a filthy pulp mill never pollutes and poisons Tasmania's Tamar Valley.

◇◇

ANNE LAYTON-BENNETT *is a published writer both in Australia and overseas. Her days are spent writing for specialist monthly magazine The Veterinarian and 50+ Tasmania magazine, and she is working on a book about the pulp mill campaign. She has also been known to pen the occasional poem – some of which have been published. She co-edited* An Inspired Pursuit: 40 years of writing by women in northern Tasmania *(Karuda Press) 2002.*

The full circle

JO VALLENTINE

The fourth of five daughters in a farming family in Western Australia, I was aware of positive role models from an early age. Both my grandfathers were community service people, and my grandmothers were articulate, well-educated women. Growing up in an all-girl family on a busy farm encouraged activities outside the usual realm of activities for girls. We all learned to do all the jobs round the farm, except milking cows. My mother drew the line at that, not wanting her daughters to miss out on social interactions because they were tied to the routine of early morning and evening milking sessions.

Convent boarding school, with daily mass over six years, made a big impact. The nuns encouraged girls to think they could do anything, but that motherhood was sacrosanct and the most important role for us. Never did they give any hints about melding a profession with motherhood – they hadn't had that experience themselves. But participation and excellence were encouraged in sports, cultural activities and in community service. Leadership skills were also strongly encouraged. My first social action, at the age of ten, was to polish other kids' shoes for three pence a pair, the proceeds going to help the missions in Africa.

Leaving school at the tender age of 16, I successfully applied for an overseas scholarship, which gave me a year in the United States representing my country. It was a mind-opening experience. Then came teachers' college, with more leadership opportunities. I was the first 'peer aged' female president of the Student Council at Graylands Teachers' College. I remember going to my first Teachers' Union conference arguing for better toilets for women. The first political challenge to the establishment, however, was not to take place until the Vietnam War Moratorium marches when, as a new teacher in 1967, I made sure that I was in the middle of the crowd so as not to be caught by television cameras.

It was travelling the world from 1969 that finally set me on an activist trajectory. I saw that the Catholic Church was not exactly a progressive force on the global stage, although I have always continued to appreciate my Loreto education. I saw poverty, over-population and pollution in so many places, and I was troubled about what the future might hold. I had discovered a new spiritual home with the Quakers and became a regular at the monthly vigils in Perth, *For disarmament East and West*. But it was actually WA Liberal Premier, Charles Court, who spurred me into full activism.

I heard him declare that 'Western Australia would be the first state in Australia to have a nuclear power station', and knowing quite a bit already about the dangers of nuclear weapons, but not much about nuclear power, I resolved to find out exactly what he was promising. One trip to the Environment Centre, to link up with the Campaign Against Nuclear Energy (CANE), and I was hooked. I'd found my calling or, rather, it had found me.

Outstanding among the activists I met at the time was Annabelle Newbury in CANE. We are still great friends. That is a wonderful spin-off from activism: working closely with people whose values you share and whose dedication is inspiring. Friendships abound. We did all kinds of things to ensure that Charlie Court's dream was never realised, and moved on to many other aspects of the nuclear industry, particularly uranium mining. To date, we still don't have an operating uranium mine in this state.

But it was a tough issue. Nuclear tentacles are everywhere. The nuclear industry is the grand-daddy of globalisation. It's an industry loyal to its mates, with friends in high places, who still believe that the nuclear industry is some kind of answer to global warming and that soon they will find out what to do with radioactive waste. They routinely lie and cover up their mistakes until there are major accidents that cannot be ignored such as TEPCO's Fukushima nuclear plant in Japan.

In 1978, my first real campaign was to get the City of Stirling – a local government area in the northern suburbs of Perth – to declare nuclear-free zone status. That it failed didn't really matter. I was full of enthusiasm and vigour, and prepared to work hard in collaboration with a small team of fellow travellers.

I continued with activism in other organisations like the Campaign to Save Native Forests, the Aboriginal Treaty Support Group, the Council for Civil Liberties and Community Aid Abroad. I also supported campaigns on issues like opposing the death penalty, and protesting against the Government's Section 54B of the Police Act, which prevented people gathering in groups of more than three without police permission.

In 1978–1979, protests focused on Noonkanbah – a pastoral station in the Fitzroy Valley – where Premier Court was determined that AMEX Oil Company could drill for oil. The station had recently been returned to its traditional owners. He got the army to protect the convoy of trucks going to wreak their destruction, an altogether over-the-top show of power. While the drilling went ahead, the political education of Indigenous people gave rise to the first of the land councils: the Kimberley Land Council. It was great to be part of that historical episode, from a supportive 'whitefella' perspective.

So by 1984, when the Labor Party had sold out its anti-uranium mining credentials, I was well placed to be considered as a candidate for the fledgling Nuclear Disarmament Party's (NDP) campaign. To the utter amazement of most people, I got elected to the Senate. This was a most positive campaign, run largely by women worried about their children's future. For many thousands of people it was their first public outing as campaigners and their first foray into politics proper. It was exhilarating, empowering. And there was a lot to learn, fast.

However, as soon as the election result was announced, trouble began to brew. It was dismaying to discover that, in a group that had no arguments during the campaign, divisions started to appear. This was largely due to the fact that a prize had been won: a place in the Senate, with all its attendant possibilities. The Socialist Workers Party (SWP) wanted to exert influence on the new, naive senator, to progress their more wide-ranging agenda.

The NDP's agenda had been very simple. It was a single-issue party with three platforms: no uranium mining, no nuclear warship visits and no foreign military bases in Australia. I felt obliged to stick to that agenda in my first term; that was what people had voted for. However, the SWP had other ideas, and while I privately agreed with many of their demands, such as social justice in places like Nicaragua and more equitable distribution of resources, I certainly didn't agree with their revolutionary methodology. They were present in large numbers at the first national meeting of the NDP, in Melbourne in April 1985, before I had actually taken my place in the Senate. In NSW and Victoria, the NDP campaigns were dominated by hard-working SWP members. They wanted the spoils of victory.

The large party meeting dissolved into chaos, which was highly embarrassing to say the least. As senator-elect I had some tough decisions to make. I was being advised by people from all over the country, among them a former Liberal member of parliament, Edward St John, who was waving around a constitution for a new green party as the walkout of the Melbourne meeting occurred, and also Peter Garrett, who had been an NDP candidate for NSW. People in other states had realised beforehand what I had not, that the NDP, with its very loose structure and its welcome to members of other political parties, was not viable.

We had a plebiscite of the 800 members in WA, who decided overwhelmingly that I should cut my links with the NDP and take my place as an independent senator for nuclear disarmament.

So the fastest growing political party in Australia's history up to that time (and probably still, despite Clive Palmer's efforts), gathering over 8000 members between July and December 1984, imploded at its first national meeting. It was a cartoonists' field day.

After re-assessing, recovering and trying to placate those West Australian voters who felt betrayed – after having given so much to this new way of doing politics and finding old divisions robbing them of the full pleasure of having their senator represent a national party – it was a time for figuring how to manage being an independent while keeping strong contact with local supporters.

An accountability group was formed, Peace and Nuclear

Disarmament Action (PANDA), which functioned for three years or so, until the next election loomed. When our Senate office was finally set up in July 1985, we managed community-based campaigns and opened the doors to other groups campaigning on social justice and environmental concerns. I always considered myself more of a community educator than a politician. Certainly we did things very differently from other political offices, sharing salaries and positions, and using the electorate allowance solely for campaign purposes.

I served eight years as a senator, having been re-elected twice, in 1987 and 1990. By the third time, we had managed to forge a Greens (WA) party, gathering in various groupings that had run in WA elections.

Always considering myself an activist who happened to get into the Senate, I continued with grassroots work, getting arrested several times and spending time in gaol. This was anathema to my Senate colleagues, who were highly resentful of my un-senatorial behaviour, and probably also resentful about the publicity I managed to attract, highlighting the issues which most of them in major parties would have preferred never to see the light of day. But I was proud to take my non-violence into the workplace, and to stand up for my beliefs.

Of course, I made lots of speeches in the Senate, asked hundreds of questions, did some work on committees, and even had some changes made to the way things operated there. Then there were the opportunities to speak with decision-makers of the day, and to work with others across party lines, like the Amnesty International group in Parliament, and the East Timor support group among many others. I was usually the token woman, and the token non-major party person on the office-bearer lists. The best bit was getting one of the coveted spots on the Joint Foreign

Affairs, Trade and Defence Committee as the first woman to be admitted. And, in the Defence sub-committee, I was a thorn in the side of the usual approach of supporting all things military, and gloating over the latest purchases of hardware. I always asked why and in what scenario could we possibly need long-range jet fighters. Always, of course, with a view to exposing the military alliance with the United States, which has pushed Australia into several wars, and all kinds of unnecessary expenditure and unwise liaisons.

Since leaving the Senate in 1992, I have gone full circle, reviving my activities in small groups, where change ultimately originates. I have co-organised some major events, like the Pilgrimage Round Australia in 1997, with two Russians from the Chernobyl-affected area on board. That same year we formed the WA branch of the Jabiluka Action Group (JAGWA). JAG was formed to protest the development of a proposed uranium mine inside the Kakadu National Park in the Northern Territory. I participated in the 1998 blockade there. In 2002, I co-organised a trip through the desert to Pine Gap, and went on to help form the Alternatives to Violence Project in WA, which offers empowering workshops in prisons, schools and the community. Then there's service for my Quaker community, which is an important anchor in my life. Also, keeping People for Nuclear Disarmament jogging along (formed in 1982) and the Anti-Nuclear Alliance of WA (since 1998), which has managed, with its partners, to prevent uranium mining occurring in this state. In the last decade I have become increasingly concerned about climate change and I have worked with various groups on this issue.

These days I see my role as mentoring the next generation of activists. I am so thrilled to see great young people stepping forward with energy and skills that are beyond me.

The major concerns facing humanity are all related, of course. One of my abiding teachers in all this activism, from the heart and soul, is Joanna Macy, a US environmentalist activist whose workshops I have attended over many years. Truly an inspiring woman, it is to her notions that I return when the going gets tough and despair seems to be taking over. Always go back to gratitude. There is so much that is beautiful and so many people working to protect our fragile planet. Joanna's latest book, *Active Hope – How to make sense of the mess we're in without going crazy*, says it all.

◇◇

JO VALLENTINE *is a peace activist, community campaigner and a former senator for Western Australia. She was included in the list of 1000 women nominated for the 2005 Nobel Peace Prize, and was nominated by the* West Australian *newspaper in 2006 to be in the list of WA's 100 most influential people. Jo is married to Peter Fry. They have two daughters and live in Perth.*

Coming home to the spirit of the land

GEORGINA WILLIAMS

I was born the eldest of 15 children in 1940 and grew up at Point Pearce Mission Station on the Yorke Peninsula in South Australia.

My father's father, Willy Boy, as he was commonly known by the old people of the Mission, was a descendant of the southern Kaurna of the Adelaide plains. Willy Boy was a fisherman and a boat builder, and my father and his brother – born at Point Pierce – carried on these roles and learned about their traditional lands. My father showed me his clan lands of Willunga and Aldinga, stretching down to the Nangkiparinga River and beyond.

On my mother's side was my Narungga grandfather, Joe Edwards. He was the great grandson of old King Tommy. My earliest childhood memory is the smell of phenol, used at the hospital for disinfectant where I was born, and at the Mission when I came home ('cleanliness is next to Godliness'), and me crying and screaming a lot, wanting to get away from it. My Narungga Papa Joe would come and take me outside into the wind and I would calm down. That's when I bonded to my papa. I spent my early childhood among the last of the old people, who by the time I was twelve had all passed away. These were the old people left behind as child survivors of the great waves of death that came sweeping over all of our traditional lands with the farmer, the axe and the plough, as we were forcibly removed from our Aboriginal life and locked into Mission life under the *Aboriginal Protection Act*.

The fathers of my two grandmothers were Tom and Tim Adams. They were the sons of a Kaurna woman, Kudnarto, who was the first Aboriginal woman legally to marry a white settler, Thomas Adams, in 1848. That was twelve years after the invasion by British colonists. When they married, under British law, Kudnarto took up a land grant specifically set aside for Aborigines by the government of the day. The land they were given was at Skillogalee in the Clare Valley. Kudnarto died seven years later at the age of 23. The land, which was held in trust for the family by the government, was taken away from Thomas Adams, and was later leased and then sold to white settlers. Kudnarto's two young sons were sent to the Poonindie Mission near Port Lincoln.

Poonindie Mission became a successful farming venture run by the Kaurna and other Aboriginal people driven from their lands and placed there, often at the point of a gun. Tom Adams became well known in the area for his farming skills and with his father and brother tried to regain the lost lands of Skillogalee over many years, but did not succeed. Our family was denied access to the land given to Kudnarto under British law. We have never been allowed to capitalise on our inheritance.

By decree of the Protector of Aborigines, the Poonindie Mission was closed in 1894 and the fertile land leased to white settlers. My family and others were dispossessed once again and forced to move to the new Mission at Point Pearce.

It was here their children grew to young adults. It was here that I was born and spent my childhood learning about the old ways. I listened to the old stories and Papa Joe and Granny Suzie always encouraged me and Mally Boy to learn by working things out for ourselves while they guided us in the right direction.

My working life for wages began when I was nine. I cleaned the school classrooms for two shillings and sixpence. By the time I was 14, I was working for a family in Minlaton, looking after a baby whose mother had meningitis, and I continued to work for families in the area. When I turned 16, Mrs Harvey, who ran the general store at Pine Point, kept telling me I didn't have to be just a Mission girl all my life. I told her I'd like to be a nurse. She arranged for me to do nursing training at the Ardrossan Hospital.

Growing up on the Mission taught me that the life around us had no balance. Everything was oriented to the whitefellas. I remember when I was little, walking up to get the milk very early in the morning, billy can in my hand, wondering why those 'other' people lived in such a big house with no children in it and why some of our women had to clean it for them.

Moving from the Mission to Adelaide was hard. We were encouraged to move because the government's policy then was assimilation. We became outcasts on the fringe of the whitefellas' society, and for a long time we needed permission to go back to visit the Mission. When I first arrived I tried lots of jobs and got involved in the three As: Aboriginal Advancement Activities, the first Aboriginal organisation in South Australia. My cousin Winifred Branson started it in the late 1950s to early 1960s. There were social gatherings where we helped each other in the unfamiliar environment. We also worked hard to raise funds to support an Aboriginal football team. I was the organiser of social events. Then I got a job as a blue nurse's aid at the infectious diseases hospital, and helped other Nunga girls get jobs there too.

My mother, Mary Williams, saw how lonely and isolated many people were. She got involved in setting up a place where Nunga parents and children could meet. This became the Alberton Kindergarten and is still going today as the Kalaya Children's Centre. My mother was always considered an activist from her days on the Mission. I've followed in her footsteps.

I've been involved over the years in all of the Aboriginal organisations here. This included the Aboriginal Housing Funded Unit, originally designed to house us in our cultural context so we could live as Aboriginal people. This has now been taken over by the public housing authority with no recognition of our cultural needs.

In the 1970s, I was a student at the Aboriginal Community College, the Aboriginal Task Force at the old South Australian Institute of Technology, and the Centre for Aboriginal Studies in Music (CASM).

At Community College I met and talked with linguists about recovering the almost extinct Kaurna language. I wanted to work on this at Batchelor College in the Northern Territory, where I could have had access to accommodation for me and my four kids while training in linguistics. But none of the other Kaurna students were interested, and the education policy at the time required at least six students before a course like this could be started. Now my cousin Lewis is working with a linguist, Rob Amery, to rebuild the language and see it taught in some of our schools.

I was dissatisfied with the course at the Aboriginal Task Force and went to study ethnomusicology and guitar at CASM. It was here that I heard again the old ritual songs like my papa sang when I was a little girl, and reconnected with all I had learned as a child on the Mission. Meeting up with the Yankunytjatjara people, and learning their *Inma nyinyi*, a bird song, I learned to read the map of their country that the bird danced in, and knew that I needed to wake up my country by bringing my clan people's songs back. I needed to reconnect to the spirituality of the land of my father's people, as he'd told it to me, here on the southern Adelaide Plains where I was living.

I was coming to understand how losing our lands that held our law, our culture and our spirituality, and having to learn the whitefella ways, was killing us as surely as the diseases, the axe and the plough the settlers had brought with them. Much of the sickness and ill health we face is a direct result of being forced out of our old ways of life. It has led most of us into intergenerational poverty and the loss of our spiritual relationship with our country.

So my real life's journey – to know and share once again the Dreaming laws of the land – began. I have worked now for many years on the recovery of the law story of Tjirbruki and his ancestral Dreaming, *Munaintya*. His journey starts at a place now called Warriparinga – 'windy place by the river', takes a direct path from the Sturt River to the sea, and then follows the coast south for many miles to the end of the Fleurieu Peninsula.

In the early 1980s, I mapped the long journey of Tjirbruki all the way along the coast. We had to struggle hard to protect the first place he stopped – Tulukudangga – a natural spring at Kingston Park. The local council wanted to clear the area. Some of the elected members referred to it as a filthy swamp. Now it is protected under the Aboriginal Heritage Act.

I then turned my focus to developing our cultural activities in the area where I was living and later transported all this to Warripari, where the Warriparinga Living Kaurna Cultural Centre now stands. The Centre, with its interactive history of black and white occupation of the land since the British arrived, evolved through a long and difficult process of negotiations between our Williams clan of the Kaurna people, the Marion Council, the state government and the local community.

For me, the work has been about 'coming home' to the spirit of my place in Kaurna country, giving us the knowledge and strength we need to live with respect as the survivors of the original inhabitants of the Adelaide plains, and teaching our young people about the peace law Tjirbruki left behind for us in his journey over the country.

Our Dreaming and our knowledge have many lessons for everyone, both Aboriginal and non-Aboriginal people.

Our Aboriginal way of life was a total system of managing and farming the land. The 'hunter-gatherer' system contained our social and religious practices and gave us the opportunity to trade with other people across the country. It was never recognised by the Europeans, but it enabled us to sustain our lives for thousands of years uninterrupted, and to develop the longest continuous surviving culture in the world. We Aboriginal people are now reduced to three per cent of the total Australian population, and the Kaurna own no land as a people at all.

Everything was pristine when the British came 200 years ago. Their system created what we have today. Now we are forced to create wetlands where there were none, to clean the water so the fish can live in the gulf.

If we are all to survive we must learn again to create a sustainable future, where the sun, wind, sea and air will guide us to draw on the spirit of creation and the land we live in, so that we come to know our place in the framework of life and learn once again how to walk over country, and be a part of Tjirbruki in harmony and peace.

GEORGINA WILLIAMS *is a Senior Kaurna Woman of water – Ngankiburka-Mekauwe – and is actively involved in all the Kaurna organisations in Adelaide today. She has been instrumental in the recovery of the Kaurna language. With her children and the Williams family clan, she continues to develop and teach her culture and spirituality, in particular in relation to her father's clan country in the southern area of the Adelaide Plains.*

Is political lobbying out of fashion?

MARGARET REYNOLDS

For an old activist of the 1960s and 70s, it comes as a shock that these days many non-government organisations seem to studiously avoid political lobbying. Some even boast they are not political, as if to engage in policy debate is sinful.

What they really mean is they are not PARTY political, because the art of effective communication and persuasion in the corridors of power involves debate with all sides of politics, keeping the focus on the issue involved.

It is certainly true that non-government organisations are now much more professional and diligent in meeting business accountability standards. Many partner with government and the corporate sector to deliver significant reform projects for vulnerable communities. But have some organisations lost the passion and zeal for change as they accept government funding and comply with those eternal compliance measures?

Community organisations contribute enormously to the wellbeing of Australians and are an influential aspect of our democracy. Nevertheless, I worry that too many have been tamed by process-driven government bureaucracies that demand ever-increasing control over independent community-based organisations.

It is no coincidence that independent lobbyists are more vocal than those dependent on government funding for survival. Yet it is essential that civil society has its independence to participate in public debate about the course of policy direction. Therefore, it is important to remind ourselves of the 'bad' old days when there was no government funding and we had to rely on simple strategies to try to influence political decision-making. Of course we often failed to effect change but over time the combined efforts of activists did contribute to alter attitudes and practices.

We marched, wrote irate letters demanding change and launched petitions. There were demonstrations with banners reinforcing our messages. We aimed to be creative and imaginative in projecting our message, and we were enthusiastic advocates for our various causes.

In the 1960s, I was in the Townsville branch of the 'Save our Sons' anti-Vietnam conscription campaign, and we prepared a large number of snack pack treats for conscripts departing from the local RAAF base in Garbutt. Each pack contained fruitcake, biscuits, sweets and a carefully typed anti-conscription message. I don't recall any detail of the wording, but I certainly recall considerable debate about indicating our support at a personal level though we opposed the political policy. It's true that military guards barred our entrance but did accept the gift packs for apparent delivery. No doubt some enjoyed the treats even though I am sure the messages would have been discarded.

As a member of the Townsville Peace Committee, I was asked to join the local clergyman to present a report highlighting our reasons for opposing conscription and the Vietnam War to Prime Minister Harold Holt. We knew he was staying overnight at a beachside motel, so very early in the morning we went to the office to ask the number of his unit. Looking back from today's security conscious environment it seems amazing that there was no questioning our motives and we could have just knocked on his door.

Instead I chose a neighbouring unit. A senior adviser answered and indicated he would see if the Prime Minister was awake. A few minutes later Harold Holt appeared in his pyjamas and tweed dressing gown to accept our protest. I can only presume there must have been a security presence nearby, but a casual observer would have just seen an affable white-haired gentleman standing in the doorway as he talked to his early morning visitors.

At the same time I was learning to use the media in an attempt to influence public opinion. As a mother of an infant son, my role in an organisation opposed to conscription of 19-year-olds had certain novelty value, so I found myself interviewed by local television and radio. It was harder to gain the attention of the local newspaper. I fronted the editor with my carefully drafted letter. I was shown into a chaotic smoke-filled office where a florid-faced gentleman kept me standing for several minutes before he turned his attention to my hesitant remarks as I handed over the letter. He then shouted, 'You know what I think of this?' and ripped it up in front of me.

It was certainly conscription that introduced me to activism, but it was racism and sexism that consolidated my commitment to political lobbying.

Racism in a North Queensland town was instantly recognisable and significantly influenced my future career path. I was dismayed to see such uncontrolled violence toward Aborigines and frequently observed blatant discrimination and vilification. Racism permeated so many aspects of community life. When I endeavoured to raise donations for Headstart

Kindergarten, the first pre-school program for Indigenous children, I found racial intolerance extended even to young children.

Our lobbying to gain recognition and equality for Indigenous people led to a significant two-day conference – 'We the Australians. What is to Follow the Referendum?' –which focused on practical education, health and employment initiatives that needed to be developed into government policy. But the state government was very suspicious that this was merely a left-wing plot designed to create instability. As a result, as secretary and organiser, I had my home ransacked by Special Branch and, like others, I was followed and my activities monitored. Despite these efforts to disrupt this important event, the conference attracted broad community support and participation, which helped to create a number of key Aboriginal and Torres Strait Islands organisations that continue to operate in North Queensland.

By 1970, I had become very active in the Women's Movement and began to lobby for recognition of women's rights. Through the Women's Electoral Lobby, we campaigned for women's voices to be heard in formulating government policy. I lobbied the local council to form a Women's Advisory Committee, and attended council meetings to find out just how decisions affecting our community were being made. We successfully lobbied the Whitlam Government for the introduction of key policies that recognised Australian women. Between 1972 and 1975 a number of policies were introduced with sex education, family planning, childcare, women's pensions, family law, women's refuges and equal pay placed firmly on the political agenda.

While we welcomed many of these developments in Queensland, we were stuck in the old world where the state government placed no priority on gender policy. In the lead up to the 1974 state election we held the Women's Electoral Lobby Cocktail Party and Forum, inviting the candidates (yes, they were all male) to come and debate their party's policies. Over 100 women of all ages dressed up for the occasion and most of the candidates attended to be questioned. The speeches were predictably devoid of any understanding of our key issues and many were prefaced by a somewhat belligerent, 'Now you ladies ...'

The questioning was impressive, as women articulated their priorities and sought responses from the men who wanted to represent them in parliament. I am not sure we changed many attitudes that night and the same old state government was returned for another term. However, we certainly had our eyes opened to what needed to be done in the future if we were to progress reform. That night made quite an impression and as a result a number of us joined political parties and began to consider nominating for preselection as candidates.

I was also involved in several environmental campaigns to prevent inner-city parkland being concreted for car parking. My first effort was as a teacher who organised parents and students to march around the park opposite our school. The march was televised and council plans were abandoned.

Our second campaign was unsuccessful, but is nevertheless an example of lobbying to create a debate about policy direction. Council was determined to build an inner-city highrise car park on riverside parkland. We formed an action group and armed with shovels and plants made our statement by planting trees where the car park was to be built. The police arrived to arrest protestors for damaging public property, but we had a lawyer among our ranks who successfully argued there was not a law against planting trees. Many years later the car park was closed and became inner-city housing.

Later, when trying to establish a North Queensland community radio station, we experienced frustration with Canberra-based bureaucracy processing the application. Despite letters and phone calls, our paperwork seemed to be lost in the system. We considered our options to gain attention from the distant north. It was suggested that it was possible to use Australia Post to send coconuts south. So we commenced an almost daily trip to the local GPO to forward a coconut to the relevant government department as a reminder of our application. After only a few weeks we received an exasperated phone call telling us to stop sending coconuts, as our application would be finalised in the near future.

By the 1980s I was myself on the receiving end of some very effective lobbying, as by this stage I had been elected to the Senate. During 16 years I witnessed national and international lobbying campaigns that generated debate and communicated policy reform to a wider audience.

I also watched my eldest daughter Anna and her friends lampoon the Queensland Labor Cabinet as they highlighted the double standard of male parliamentarians pronouncing against abortion law reform. They held a silent vigil outside a conference to consider decriminalisation of abortion. The students, dressed formally but with the aid of cushions and photo masks, clearly identified the ministry as 'the pregnant cabinet', an image too amusing for local media to ignore. Twenty years later the Queensland government still needs to be lobbied for this particular reform.

I certainly can attest to the fact that political lobbying is frustrating and often may fail to get results. But that is no reason to abandon the process. It is an essential feature of the community's participation in our democracy. And who knows when suddenly an idea whose time has come will be accepted as official policy or best practice? So by all means continue with the professional presentation of facts and figures, but do remember that a creative lobbying strategy is often the one that makes the best impression for reform.

MARGARET REYNOLDS *has spent over 40 years working for women's equality and social justice reform here and internationally. She is a former Labor senator. In 2007 she wrote her autobiography* Living Politics.

From workplace to saving the beaches

JIM DOUGLAS

I was born in 1943 in a suburban home on the Esplanade at Brighton, a seaside suburb of Adelaide. My parents were working class and lived most of their married life in public housing. Dad was a munitions worker during the Second World War and later became a motorman, driving trams and buses for the Municipal Tramways Trust. Mum was the backbone of the family, working part-time jobs and giving a great deal of her time to the community.

My parents always voted for the Labor Party and worked hard at election time winning votes for ALP candidates. They disliked the prime minister, Robert Menzies, and would sit my young sister and me alongside the big old HMV radio to listen to Menzies getting stuck into the ALP, with Dad screaming at the radio, 'That's right. Find another red under the bed, you silly bastard.' I didn't really understand all this yelling until I started work as an apprentice fitter and machinist at the Islington Railway Workshops in 1959.

I joined the left-wing Amalgamated Engineering Union (AEU) on my second day at work, after listening to two shop stewards from different engineering unions telling us what they could do to protect our interests in the workplace. The AEU bloke mentioned how much he disliked Menzies and the other bloke talked about getting on well with the boss. There is no second-guessing why I joined the AEU.

It didn't take long to become involved in the union movement, because an apprentice got lousy pay and had to attend night school for four hours a week without being paid. Something had to be done to improve our conditions.

I soon became the apprentices' representative on the combined unions' Workshop Committee, and was encouraged to attend political economy schools at weekend camps, where I listened to activists from other workplaces as well as from overseas. I read a lot about workers' struggles and what communism and socialism was all about.

I was married at 18 and we had three children by the time we were 23, two boys and a girl. It was hard work and we had very little money, but we managed to save £50 (about $100) that gave us a deposit on a Housing Trust rental-purchase home at Elizabeth West, in the new northern suburbs. We were surrounded by English and European migrants who had much more experience than we did of family living and what was needed to bring the community together.

The Workshop Committee at Islington consisted of 16 different unions representing trades and semi-skilled workers. There were over 1500 workers from 40 countries with varying political circumstances, and all had to be taken into consideration. If we were organising a factory gate meeting, a rally for wages and conditions, or encouraging people to rally against the Vietnam War, every action required long and strategic planning. How do we get a message to workers when English is their second or third language? We could not rely on a newsletter or a large meeting. We began to form hubs or circles of friends to speak one-on-one to as many as we could so that they understood what we were asking them to become involved in. It took great patience and listening skills. Often things would become heated and aggressive. I always remembered to place my hands in my pockets and never become aggressive in return.

Gradually, everything was beginning to make sense from what I was learning on the workshop floor, the interactions with people from other countries, the readings, a sense of community, and the need to think, feel, organise and act.

After 20 years on the shop floor I became a national organiser and industrial officer for the Construction Forestry Mining Energy Union (CFMEU). That took me to most states where I advocated for workers rights, and was involved with dispute resolution and the Industrial Commission and Court. It was hard work, with long hours, endless plane flights, sleepless nights reading and preparing, and frightening confrontations with our own members over various forestry operations and industrial building practices. It certainly tested my environmental beliefs and passion.

In 1993, after a car accident and long recovery, I decided to quit full-time paid work. Thus began my community involvement once again, this time in the seaside area where I now lived. I became the president of my local residents' association.

In 1996, the South Australian Government announced it was going to create a major development at Glenelg, to be known as Holdfast Shores, on the western Adelaide coastline. To enable them to do this they needed to transfer community land to crown land, build massive rock wall groynes out into the Gulf St Vincent, relocate a number of small community clubs, and redirect massive volumes of polluted storm water through a huge pipeline called the Barcoo Outlet into the sea. All the science would tell them that this plan was going to create huge problems by depleting the northern beaches of sand, eroding the remnant dune system and lowering the sea bottom. Millions of dollars would need to be spent in perpetuity if Adelaide's beaches were to be maintained for recreational purposes.

Soon after this announcement a community action group of 16 was set up to organise a campaign to save our beaches. We all knew it would be a hard task to turn the government position around, but we knew we had to make a stand.

Our first task was to inform the three communities we believed would be most directly affected. This meant publishing and then letterboxing over 10,000 information leaflets letting people know what we had learnt from the science and practical experiences of long time residents. It was followed up with a public meeting of over 500 people at the Henley Beach Town Hall where over 400 people gave a 'pledge' to join the Save Our Beaches campaign.

In 1998, a 24-hour vigil was set up on the main road leading to the construction site, waiting for the work to commence. We erected large signage inviting the passing cars and people to stop and listen to our story and, at the same time, join the campaign. In total over 600 people signed the pledge.

We set up an elaborate Phone Tree with five levels of contact. We gave each group the name of a bird that identified their group responsibilities. The Action Committee were the Owls, the primary decision-makers, and they contacted the Chief Pelicans. The Chief Pelicans contacted the Pelicans and they contacted the Seagulls. In this way, we could get information out to our supporters very rapidly. There was also the support group who would provide the food and drinks and entertainment. They were the Terns.

After many sessions of non-violent action training we were ready to take action.

When the construction was about to start we held our first blockade and over 300 people linked arms and turned the trucks back. This ongoing action took place for five days in succession, usually at around 7 to 9 am, when the trucks would back away.

In between all our actions we were lobbying politicians. We made a media release every night and had direct contact with various TV and radio journalists, advising them what new action we were about to take. Every day we took a different action to keep the group together and keep the media interested in the story: we dressed in black; we wore bandannas and masks. Community singing went down a treat, and each day we dedicated a new conductor. A home-made boiled fruit cake arrived every second day, baked by a dear woman aged ninety who wanted to be part of the blockade, but no longer had the energy. We assured her that we needed the energy of her wonderful cake to keep going.

We made presentations to local councils seeking their support and we held two major fundraisers: an art auction and a live music concert. The proceeds enabled us to produce our information as full page advertisements in the Adelaide *Advertiser* and the local suburban newspapers.

We did a skills audit of all members of the campaign group so that we could utilise their skills. We found engineers, doctors of medicine, nurses, school teachers, information technicians, builders, labourers, clerks, counsellors, and, best of all, great cooks.

As the blockade became more determined, the force shown by the police to move us on increased. Quite severe and painful tactics were used by the police to break the blockade. However, it stood strong on 42 occasions until we could no longer sustain the physical effort.

We took on the establishment but they were too strong and there weren't enough of us to stop the destruction that we are experiencing today. The West Beach dunes have eroded and two metres of sand have gone from the beachfront. Millions of dollars are spent each year to dredge the boat harbours at Glenelg and West Beach. The storm water is polluting Gulf St Vincent. The Environmental Protection Authority recently issued a warning that no one is to swim in the Gulf waters for three days after rain.

It was a hard-fought campaign that involved many strategies and tactics. Without any question it developed for many people a far greater awareness and understanding of the importance of standing up for what you believe is right.

My years as a union organiser had taught me many things. Working at the local community level has taught me many more.

- Tactics and creative thinking are critical components of any action and most of the best ideas and actions come from the workers or the community involved.
- We must never lose faith in the belief that we can make things change to get a fair go, providing we don't allow our egos to overtake common sense and demand things that are not possible to achieve
- Always be alongside of the people and never go too far in front where you lose touch with them.

People know instinctively if something is unfair or wrong. The greatest challenge for us all is how to change that idea into the courage, the passion and the wisdom that enables us to act to make a change for the better.

JIM DOUGLAS *continues to be active in his local community as President of the Western Adelaide Coastal Resident Association. In 2013 he received the Premier's Natural Resource Management Award for community engagement.*

The resilience and 'stickability' of the artist

ANNE RIGGS

I think I have always had a strong sense of fairness and justice. I doubt it can be otherwise in a large family. Although my mother vehemently claimed, 'I am not a feminist!' her two sons were given the same domestic chores as her five daughters and, as there were seven of us, each child was allocated one day per week for dishes, table-setting and cleaning duties.

My parents are kind people. In the days when cars were not as ubiquitous as now, my father shared his. He picked up and delivered kids to school, drove a little boy with a disability and his family to church; he ferried and carted people where he saw need and could help. These parents, as guides, were not demonstrating ways to effect change as much as ways to treat others, ways to meet people with kindness and as equals, and to assist where you can be useful.

My mother is quite a shy person, who often retreated behind the large and affable personality of my father. Nonetheless, we were brought up to believe that we could choose, pursue and achieve our own goals, whatever they may be. Education was important, so too resilience, and that we stick with a task until its completion – values that were underpinned by our school. I still remember one teacher inculcating us with the concept of 'stickability', of not giving up.

Alongside creativity, resourcefulness and technical know-how, resilience and stickability are essential qualities for the artist.

I don't think I ever set out to be an activist or to effect change. I started working with vulnerable people because I needed to earn money. However, I soon discovered the profound impact of creativity, of the relationships between artist and participants, and the power of bringing people together to create a community. Through art, I saw people who had lost their way through poverty, mental illness, disability, trauma and poor education find a renewed sense of self and of purpose through art making.

I felt great pleasure in passing on my art skills, and breaking down tasks into manageable chunks so that each person could grasp them and succeed. I enjoyed the exchanges and seeing participants escape the constraints that had shaped their lives.

Dishearteningly, for all the wondrous things I saw and heard in these art groups, I found I was forever spruiking the benefits of art and creative practice. I tormented organisations to fund arts programs and tried to convince them, and friends, that artists and participation in creative practices really do have an immense and positive influence on people's lives. I tired of the responses: 'Wouldn't that money be better going into hospitals or schools?' No, it wouldn't. All require proper financial support, and arts programs, when properly conceived, funded and delivered by artists, are extremely cost-effective in keeping people well, in education, in work, in the community, out of hospitals, out of trouble, away from detrimental drinking habits, off prescribed and non-prescribed medication, alive, and leading meaningful lives.

Yes, I know, that sounds incredible and rather fanciful. Nonetheless, it's true. One of the purposes I had for undertaking a PhD was to 'prove' the efficacy of artist-led community arts programs. Another was exploring how artists contribute to community wellbeing through the interpretation of the world around us, focusing on difficult human emotional states and experiences. Artists make the unviewable viewable, the unbearable bearable, and are a conduit to deeper self-reflection and understanding.

Our artist's practice is crucial in informing our community work, which in turn can inform our practice. The roles interweave. In order to understand how the arts are effective in community development, wellbeing and education, it is essential to grasp the pivotal function of the artist.

I undertook my research with women victims of sexual assault, teaching them mosaic making, as well as working with clay and expressing their grief, loss and emotions such as anger and revenge. In these creative spaces, and later in similar spaces with victims of family violence, women who had been abused, humiliated, and treated with contempt revealed the heartbreaking and long-term effects of the abuse. They had been robbed of their innocence, the chance to enjoy sensuality and sexuality, and to express and use their voice. The abuse dissolved into mental illness, drug and alcohol dependence, poor relationship choices, poor work opportunities, self-harm and suicide. I was appalled.

Yet, as a result of their participation, I saw women, and later men and children, flourish. Their creativity, self-esteem, social connectedness, capacity to enjoy life and to trust others all increased as depression, anxiety, self-loathing, alcohol and drug dependence and negative feelings diminished.

Now, whether the opportunity arises or not, I speak about abuse, especially childhood maltreatment and sexual abuse. I speak of the effects it can have upon a person for the rest of their lives, and of our responsibilities to the vulnerable in our community. I also speak of the wonder of arts practice, the resilience of victims, and their desire to create and live a better life.

I work closely and collaboratively with individual participants to showcase their creativity in exhibitions, publications, conferences and on the internet. These gentle inroads into the public sphere are effective in bringing awareness of sexual assault and family violence in ways that are viewable and, therefore, discussable. They also reveal a positive message by showing these survivors of abuse are also creative, thoughtful and intelligent people who demonstrate there is hope and a future after negative and debilitating experiences.

Years ago, when I was teaching at the Victorian College of the Arts in Melbourne, a steady stream of artists and guests from all over the world visited the College. They volunteered their time to share their experiences and skills with students. This ignited a spark within me to volunteer at an arts project in Calcutta with my partner and performing artist Alex Pinder, when we travelled to India in 2005.

Since then we have established Artists in Community International (AICI). It's a small organization whose aim is to reclaim the value that artists and the arts bring to community life. We wanted to create an organisation that would inspire and educate communities, individuals and leaders to be creative in and through art making. We wanted to expose them to all sorts of arts and to the creative thinking we have discovered on our journey as arts makers.

AICI provides creative programs to those who would otherwise be unlikely to experience the joy, fun, challenges and expression that the arts bring. We see this as an exhilarating way to enter the life of a community. We strive to offer engaging programs that are inclusive, challenging and dynamic, and which have long-term benefits to education, health, community and individual development.

We have worked in Thailand, India and Nepal, as well as Australia. We've facilitated arts programs in a wide range of situations including village communities, schools, a girls' home, with internally displaced persons, tribal people, the sick, the deaf, street children, sex workers, and community leaders. All participants know or have known significant hardship, prejudice and suffering; most have or are being treated poorly by others. They do not expect to be heard or valued and have neither expectation nor opportunity to express their individuality, creativity or opinions.

The many stark inequities we see could overwhelm us. But we are not demoralised. Instead, we choose to do what is within our capacity and what we know to be effectual. Our art and drama programs impart arts-practice knowledge, as well as provide a range of other skills and benefits. We believe that one of our greatest contributions, beyond this, is the collaborative and equal relationship between us as facilitators. We work in many communities where women and girls have a much lower status than men and boys. By demonstrating our equal partnership we provide excellent role models for both sexes.

Alex and I each bring our unique suite of skills to a project, as well as shared skills in project development and facilitation. Among the benefits and joys of collaboration are the new spaces that open up as our individual skills meet and enable new processes and creative journeys to evolve. This meeting is particularly useful in creating new art works around shared and often difficult themes for participants, such as looking and working with the human body in processes that include observational exercises, physical movements and drawing, sculpture or painting.

Art in the community reaches out to connect with the humanness of those who are often collectively bundled together as 'people in developing countries', street children, or the mentally ill. At its best, it breaks barriers that have excluded individuals from fully participating in life, and opens up spaces for them to explore, create and be.

◇◇

ANNE RIGGS *is a Melbourne-based artist who practises her art in many ways and places: in the studio, in the community, through writing and publication, teaching, community and public art projects and professional development training. She has exhibited widely.*

Turning ideas into reality in Afghanistan

MATTHIAS TOMCZAK

My wife Chris and I arrived in Australia from Germany in 1979; I had a contract to work with the CSIRO in Sydney. In 1992 we moved to Adelaide, where I took up a job at Flinders University.

We have a Festival of Ideas in Adelaide. In 2004, a woman from RAWA, the Revolutionary Association of the Women of Afghanistan, spoke at the Festival. She described RAWA as an organisation that promotes a secular Afghanistan, separation of state and religion, the end of ethnic competition and rivalry, equality of all people from all ethnic groups, and equal rights for women. I remembered the revolution of Ayatollah Khomeini in Iran in 1979 and was rather suspicious of the label 'revolutionary' coming from a Muslim country. So I inquired about RAWA through the internet and found that RAWA is a democratic organisation of women, with only women members, but supported by men as well.

I see the transition of Islam from religious to secular states as one of the most important tasks for the 21st century, and believe the women's struggle for equal rights is an important aspect of that transition.

So I thought RAWA deserved support. I sent an email suggesting we establish a support group in Australia. Within hours I received a reply. I was told that a woman in Castlemaine had the same idea, and was already in the process of setting up SAWA, the Support Association for the Women of Afghanistan, in Victoria to raise support for RAWA. I linked up with her and decided to establish a support group in Adelaide.

I believe in grassroots action. I wanted to make SAWA into an organisation run and maintained by a collective of supporters. The question was, how would I find people prepared to support SAWA and join the collective?

The movie *Osama* was showing in Adelaide at the time. I made up a small flyer that said something like – I forget the exact words, it is too long ago for my fading memory – 'If you want to help the women of Afghanistan to liberate themselves from the conditions you have just seen, contact me', followed by my phone number. A dozen people, all women, responded and came to a first meeting. After a few months six or eight of them stayed on as the SAWA group for Adelaide, and took up fundraising for RAWA.

A year or so later, the people running the Castlemaine group contacted me and asked if the Adelaide group could take over the running of SAWA as they were about to take an extended holiday, touring Australia. We agreed and incorporated SAWA in South Australia in 2005. Since then our group in Adelaide has provided nearly all the members for the national SAWA committee.

One of the things SAWA organised in 2005 was a speaking tour for a RAWA member. Presenting a RAWA member to the public is not a trivial task. RAWA's demand of a secular state and separation of state and religion goes against Afghanistan's constitution, which defines the country as an Islamic republic. RAWA is, therefore, persecuted in Afghanistan. If a person or organisation is identified as having contacts with RAWA this can lead to targeted attacks. So RAWA members do not use their real names in public.

RAWA member 'Amena' travelled around Australia in 2005 sponsored by SAWA. She stayed with us in Adelaide, and we are now very close friends.

During the first three or four years, SAWA's support for the women of Afghanistan was directed toward financial support for schools and orphanages or 'foster havens', initially those run by RAWA, but later also those of other organisations.

In 2008 I travelled to Afghanistan to visit one of the foster havens run by the Afghan Child Education and Care Organisation. AFCECO was established and registered as a charity in Afghanistan in 2008. Like RAWA, AFCECO promotes the end of ethnic competition and rivalry, equality of all people from all ethnic groups and equal rights for women, but does not insist on a secular state and separation of state and religion in its documents. Through determination and initiative AFCECO's director, Andeisha Farid, managed to establish an entire network of foster havens in all major cities of Afghanistan. Most are supported by donors from the United States, but from 2005 to 2010 SAWA-Australia was playing its small part as well.

SAWA's contact with the Organisation for Promoting Afghan Women's Capabilities (OPAWC) was the result of the wish of some SAWA members to do something for the many illiterate war widows. I mentioned this to Andeisha in 2007 in various emails and discussed with her how SAWA-Australia could help them. As a result, OPAWC's Vocational Training Centre was born.

SAWA's membership and support base grew over the years, with around 120 members and more than 350 names on its supporter list. In 2010 there was sufficient support in Sydney to allow SAWA to establish itself as an incorporated association in New South Wales, and since 2011 SAWA-Australia exists as two independent associations – SAWA-Australia (SA) and SAWA-Australia (NSW). The two associations publish a joint quarterly newsletter but otherwise operate independently, with SAWA (NSW) continuing to support a RAWA school in Pakistan, while SAWA (SA) supports projects in Afghanistan.

OPAWC's Vocational Training Centre became and still is the major support project for SAWA (SA). With the help of Melbourne artist Gali Weiss and her artist colleagues, we could document our work through an ambitious and beautiful book project that combines Australian art with personal stories of Afghan women from one of its literacy classes. Publishing a book can be a drain on resources, so I had to find a way to get the printing costs covered before we began. Raising money through crowdfunding on the internet was just taking off in Australia. It was new to me, but after much deliberation and careful preparation of the campaign I managed to raise $12,000 to print 1000 copies. *Two Trees*, the resulting coffee-table book, documents the struggle of the women of Afghanistan and our support. Several hundred copies have been sold already, raising more than $17,000 for the Vocational Training Centre.

OPAWC also runs Hamoon Clinic, a health centre in remote Farah Province, and asked SAWA (SA) to help with its funding. Our donation income is not enough to come to the aid of the Clinic, but through the assistance of APHEDA, the overseas aid organisation of the trade union movement, we were able to get valuable help from Planet Wheeler, the private aid fund of the founders of Lonely Planet, Maureen and Tony Wheeler. Planet Wheeler has been funding Hamoon Clinic since 2011.

When I visited OPAWC in 2013, I was told the Hamoon Clinic was in dire need of an ambulance. I thought if people are prepared to support the printing of a book, why shouldn't they support the purchase of an ambulance for Afghanistan? I started another crowdfunding drive and, in February 2014, SAWA (SA) could send $15,000 to OPAWC to buy an ambulance. One month later it was already in service.

While I am happy with the results achieved for OPAWC, I feel that this work moved away from my own interest to support a political move from an Islamic to a secular state. When I visited Kabul in 2013, I noticed the time would soon come when the first girls in the foster havens would have finished high school and hope to go to university. Girls who come out of AFCECO's orphanages will be important members of the new Afghanistan that, hopefully, will move away from fundamentalism and ethnic rivalry. Helping them will have a much bigger impact in the political struggle than helping illiterate poor women. Not that this should be underrated; some women from the Vocational Training Centre are now teaching women's rights in their home villages. But I always hoped to support the political struggle.

AFCECO's orphanages are sponsored by supporters in the USA. I did not want to encroach on that, but when the issue of university sponsorships came up I thought that SAWA (SA) could find sponsors for a limited number of girls. Since 2012, SAWA (SA) members have sponsored some of AFCECO's girls through university scholarships.

It has, of course, been a great source of joy and satisfaction to see SAWA grow, but the need to raise nearly $100,000 every year to keep all supported projects going is also a constant cause of concern. While many people are prepared to contribute, people prepared to do the necessary footwork are sometimes thin on the ground. But SAWA (SA) has managed so far and will continue to manage somehow. The girls and women of Afghanistan deserve it.

MATTHIAS TOMCZAK *is Emeritus Professor of Oceanography at Flinders University in Adelaide. His work has taken him to all oceans and many countries, and he has experienced the contrast between our affluent world and the world of the poor. He has given lectures and workshops on care for the marine environment in Cuba, Kenya, Malta, Fiji and Thailand. His work for SAWA-Australia has been acknowledged in 2015 through a Sustaining Women's Empowerment in Communities and Organisations (SWECO) Award from the Australian Centre for Leadership for Women and through a unanimously supported resolution of the Australian Senate.*

Doing what I feared the most

JENNY SCOTT

I don't remember the exact occasion when I first heard myself described as 'an activist'. It may have been at a forum during a Feast Festival. But I do remember my surprise. An activist, I thought to myself. When did that happen?

I am now celebrating 23 years of being 'out' as a transgender person, and I am genuinely delighted to see how far transgender visibility and recognition have come in recent years. Certainly transgender people are still routinely vilified and physically and emotionally attacked, but there is growing mainstream recognition of us as a marginalised minority deserving of protection.

The experience that led others to describe me as an activist dates back 56 years to the time when I was five years old, living on an Air Force base in New Zealand. It was the Cold War. Military aircraft from Australia, the United States and the United Kingdom were regular visitors. Life on base was protected and in many ways idyllic. We were all 'Air Force brats', free to roam and enjoy the adventures and facilities that living on base provided.

But for me that was also the year I became 'closeted'. One day I innocently dressed in my mother's wedding dress and paraded into the kitchen to show her how pretty I looked. I was told to change immediately. I remember little else of the episode, and years later when I discussed it with my mother, she claimed no memory of it. Nevertheless it taught me that I should never 'dress up' again.

It did not stop me, however. When opportunities presented I continued to dress in my mother's evening gowns. I particularly remember one that was a beautiful jade-green Thai silk. For a child who is five or six or seven years old this is quite innocent and delightful play, but the years of puberty that lay ahead would bring added confusion and fear of discovery. It can be hard enough to explain the concepts of sex, sexuality and gender to an adult in the 21st century, but as a child in the mid 1960s I had to confront these on my own. My sex appeared to be unequivocally XY male, my gender identity was female, and my sexuality was lesbian! I saw in girls and later in women everything that attracted me and I admired.

This experience led me to be shy, easily embarrassed and socially awkward. It was not until 1973 when I met a young woman with whom I could speak easily that I eventually 'came out' for the second time, and told her I was a cross-dresser. To admit to myself, let alone anyone else, that I was 'transsexual' would have been too personally confronting. With acceptance came love and we married and had three daughters. I always believed, hoped and prayed that this would 'cure' me, but it didn't, and despite desperate efforts to be 'normal', my gendered self would regularly demand expression.

With time the need to be myself became increasingly urgent and I suffered a series of panic attacks and breakdowns, such that I eventually was confronted with the choice of self-harm or the ultimate frightening step: to tell myself and the world I was transgender.

I came out in 1993 while a student at the University of South Australia, studying for my graduate diploma in library and information management. As a result of this act I was surrounded by a group of wonderfully supportive women, particularly my lecturer, Dr Margaret Peters. These women and my fellow students gave me a safe and supported space in which to transition, and they became among the first of many who have shown me love and support over the past 20 years – without which I could never have been called an activist.

But to be transgender and 'out' in itself leads to a politically activist life. I have lectured often since then and believe there is no greater divide in this or any society that the human species has created than gender. No other human construct has so destined some to great power and others to great deprivation. Throughout history in families, communities, societies and nation states, with few exceptions, 'sex' and its apparently inseparable partner 'gender' have been the primary deciders of place, privilege and power.

It was my lived experience of this construct that convinced me in 1994 nothing could change for transgender people without positive visibility, visibility that would prove the lie of those who would vilify and discriminate against us.

Many of the activities I have participated in over the past 20 years have little consciously to do with my being transgender or were actively sought by me. I was honoured to be twice elected to head the Gay and Lesbian Counselling Service (GLCS) in South Australia in the mid 1990s, an experience that gave me an excellent and thorough community education. Then the Australian Democrats asked me to stand as a candidate for the Australian Senate in 2004 and the South Australian Parliament in 2006. I have participated in many community organisations and committees, including Bfriend, Feast, Gay and Lesbian Health Ministerial Advisory Council, and SA Police Equal Opportunity Consultative Forum. I was honoured to be able to work with Ian Purcell AM and his partner Stephen in the library of the AIDS Council of South Australia.

But community activism for me was never enough in itself. I always felt that being transgender was just a diagnosis, and I needed to continue to follow my passion for history and photography. My graduate qualification in information management combined with the management experience gained as President of GLCS secured me a permanent position as an archivist with State Records South Australia. In turn this led to my qualification as a professional archivist, and working with archives and photographs at the State Library of South Australia.

This passion has resulted in me being an 'activist' for archival records, presenting papers on access at national and international conferences in Australia, New Zealand and the Pacific.

These professional experiences have in recent years convinced me of the importance of moving beyond my transgender experience to reclaim the 40 years I lived before coming out. Those 40 years placed layers of gender experience on me, experiences that are part of who I am. I choose to celebrate these experiences, not deny them in order to fit some societal definition of who I should be and what I should do.

This past year I have been attending community events and remarking to my partner of 18 years how very few transgender folk I have known remain visibly active today. I wonder if there is something wrong with me that I still find a value in being a visible activist and supportive of my transgender community. Perhaps there is, but I choose to believe that there is still much to be gained by transgender community members being proud of the hurdles we have overcome just to survive, let alone flourish, in a world that would judge us.

There is immeasurably more to be gained by confronting all forms of discrimination that in the final analysis places a cost and burden on us all that is indefensible and unsustainable.

On my bedside table I keep a short anonymous poem that goes a long way to describing why I am an activist.

Hurrah!
I did the thing I feared the most.
Excuse me while I cheer.
Now here I stand a stronger soul,
And all I've lost is fear.

◇◇

JENNY SCOTT *is an archivist and librarian at the State Library of South Australia. In 2012 she published* Dumbo Diary, *a wartime history of her father's Catalina squadron in the Pacific. In 2016 she and her partner, Anthea Smith, celebrated 20 years together. Jenny's personal archive has been accepted for inclusion in the collection of the State Library.*

Where volunteering can lead you

JOHN BENNETT

Suddenly I was in my 70th year on the planet. I'd never wanted to retire from active work. I thoroughly enjoyed my life as a building project manager. I had a good social life, many friends, and I was living and working in the tropics. However, thoughtless others believed I had passed my use-by date and it was time to wish 'old John' a sad goodbye. I was dragged kicking and screaming into retirement, and became another reluctant retiree on the scrap heap.

I saw no sense in wasting my remaining years as a cynical old bore at the local RSL or bowling club, boring everyone to death mumbling about my previous experiences ranging from a miserable childhood at a Catholic school, my enlistment in the Australian Army, which saw me walking around the ruins of the atomic-bombed Hiroshima at 17, to commanding a platoon of soldiers in Korea when I was 22. Who would want to listen when my dialogue would drift into my life and experience of fourteen years in the Pacific? Of course most people my age have tales of their own experiences in life, to which I would readily switch off.

When my wife and I returned from the Pacific we both became involved with the local Circle of Friends, an apolitical, non-religious group that supports refugees in the community. At the time, the Circle was actively involved in skirmishes with the then Coalition government in their treatment of refugees who had arrived onshore by boat, and were held in various immigration detention centres in Australia.

Along with many others, we had visited the Baxter Detention Centre – some 200 kilometres north of Adelaide. I was familiar with the place when it was a largely unfenced army training camp, but was staggered to see a new two-metre-high chain mesh fence topped with razor wire, and electrically charged. There was a gap of 30 metres to a two-metre-high inner chain-mesh fence. These men behind the wire were not criminals. In fact, all were later found to be genuine refugees to whom Australia had an international obligation to protect.

I think the sight of the electric fences, the absurd security, and the general indifference of the guards firmed my resolve to do whatever I could to assist refugees. What was my country doing to these people?

I clearly had forgotten the good army maxim: Never volunteer for anything.

Following a change of government and a softening of policy toward the so-called 'boat people', those who had originally been given a temporary protection visa could apply for a permanent protection visa. A call had come out from the South Australian Legal Service for volunteers to sit in on cases that were being held by the Immigration Department to establish if people on temporary protection visas still required protection. If it was found that protection was still required, their status was changed from temporary to permanent protection. This change meant they would be able to apply to bring their spouses and children to Australia to join them. I agreed to become a voluntary support person.

Sitting in at the interview and taking detailed notes of the proceedings ensured transparency and no bias by the assessing officer. It also enabled an independent person to advise a refugee where he may not have clearly articulated his continuing need for protection. It was sobering to hear of the tragic circumstances of these men fleeing terror in their own country.

In 2007, one of our Afghan friends, Sayeed,† talked to us about his concerns for his brother Kailil who, at 12 years of age, had witnessed the torture and execution of their mother by the Taliban. He was then thrown into a Taliban prison for two years before he was released upon the American invasion of Afghanistan. Through the efforts of Sayeed and the Australian Red Cross Tracing Service, Kailil was found in Iran. Sayeed approached a registered migration agent and paid him to lodge the necessary papers to enable his brother to join him in Australia. The visa application was rejected, but the applicant was given the right of appeal. The migration agent then acted negligently by failing to lodge the necessary appeal within the time limit, despite myself and Sayeed urging him to act. The appeal period lapsed without any chance of a review.

I referred the matter to the Migration Registration Review Board immediately, and began a very lengthy correspondence with both the Immigration Department and the responsible minister at the time, Chris Evans. The Migration Registration Review Board subsequently suspended the agent. Finally, the minister saw the injustice and granted Kailil permanent protection.

Kailil flew out of Islamabad to Adelaide as soon as he was given his visa. Two days later he came to my home to thank me

---

† Real names have not been used

for helping him. I was very emotional. This 22-year-old man had endured much at the hands of the Taliban and brigands on the Turkish border, who had threatened to cut out his kidneys unless his brother in Australia paid them $US5000. He was very thin, but within days started to exercise and attend a local library to improve his English. He now lives in Perth where he is working as a carpenter. This year he will become a registered builder.

Soon after, Sayeed began wondering what could be done to help the three orphaned children of his uncle, who had been executed along with Sayeed's mother. Fatima was 12, Zabibullah was 10, and Ali was eight. The children were being cared for by an elderly couple in Afghanistan who were in declining health.

Following discussions with a local immigration officer, it was suggested that I act as an authorised recipient and apply for a humanitarian visa on their behalf. But the path is never easy. The immigration officer in Islamabad rejected the application for spurious reasons, despite declarations by village officials of frequent Taliban raids in the village where the children resided, during which they took boys and girls captive. The immigration officer suggested a humanitarian visa could not be granted since the girl could be married off, as is the custom in that country. It was such an offensive suggestion, made by an officer who had the power to make decisions against which there was no appeal. He had failed to consider a request, before making his decision, that he discuss the matter with Sayeed, who was by now an Australian citizen. He also ignored direction by the Supreme Court of Afghanistan that Sayeed, as the sponsor and cousin of the children, was to be their legal guardian.

Incensed by this response, I arranged a meeting with the Minister for Immigration, Senator Evans, who listened and then instructed the Director of Immigration to 'fix the problem'.

Easier said than done. To fix the problem meant another visa classification at an estimated cost of $5000, plus likely additional costs if the matter proceeded to other tribunals.

Since the local Circle of Friends had no such funds and were unlikely to raise such a large amount, I approached Sister Pat Sealey, a Josephite nun who, as a Registered Migration Agent, undertook pro bono work. In asking for her help, I suggested that in return I could assist with the administration of the office and any chores she needed done. I don't think she was terribly impressed with my administrative ability, but still agreed to do the work pro bono.

Sister Pat applied for an orphan relative visa and after five years of hard work the children were granted permanent protection. Sayeed immediately flew to Afghanistan to collect them. The local villagers had managed to avoid Taliban roadblocks and got the children safely to Kabul.

We went to Adelaide Airport to meet three tired but very happy young people. When Fatima and her two brothers walked over to me, knelt and kissed my extended hand as a token of their gratitude, I felt humbled, but also proud that the past five years of my life had been so usefully rewarding. Sayeed said quietly, 'John, you have given my brother and now these three children a new life.' The children are all at school and doing extremely well, and keep in touch with us.

Now I head off to Sister Pat's office once a week to put away any completed files, and get to work with vacuum, mop and detergent. When I found that she was always too busy to eat lunch, I began to bring her one, ranging from soup in the winter to sandwiches and strawberries in summer. After all, she is not that much younger than me!

When my local town held a 'Walk Through Willunga' event

eight years ago and someone called for a volunteer to clean shoes, I seemed to be the obvious choice. I've had a lifetime of shoe cleaning. It's become a regular fixture every Saturday between April and October. Our charity shoe cleaning has raised hundreds of dollars for Ethiopian projects and refugees in Afghanistan.

So at 85 years of age, I have avoided becoming the old bore in the club. I have metamorphosed, becoming just the 'Grumpy Old Man' sitting under a green-shaded tent each Saturday morning, speaking endlessly about refugee issues while cleaning and polishing footwear.

Perhaps that old sergeant was wrong after all when he warned new recruits never to volunteer for anything.

◇◇

JOHN BENNETT *retired from active work as a building project manager to take up active voluntary work in support of refugees. John has just learned that his friend Sayeed's youngest brother, who was 10 years old when his mother was executed and believed to have been killed by the Taliban the same day, has been located in Turkey. So John's work looks to continue despite his protestations.*

First Footprints *in every primary school*

MADDISON DAY

I am 12 years old and live in the suburb of Valley View in Adelaide. At the time of writing I had just finished my primary schooling at Paradise Primary School. When it comes to heritage and culture, I am a real mixed bag. My mum is half Italian and half English, and my dad is half German and half Aboriginal. These are only the major parts. There are more, some known and some unknown.

I am not sure why but I have always been drawn to the Aboriginal part of me. I find the history and culture of Aboriginal people intriguing and it makes me eager to learn more about it. This year we had an Aboriginal Education Worker come to schools to work with Aboriginal students and teach us about our culture. I was the only Indigenous student from Paradise so I went to another primary school to have lessons with students of Aboriginal descent. I was immediately interested and enthusiastic. Projects were a pleasure to do and learning about our culture was fun and interesting.

During these lessons we had to present our Aboriginal family tree. I really enjoyed working on the project with my dad and learning about my family. We also did a project on David Unaipon who is on the $50 note. Not only did I learn what an amazing person he was for his time, but that he is also from the Ngarrindjeri tribe, the same as me.

I didn't know it but my school nominated me for a National Aborigines and Islanders Day of Observance Committee (NAIDOC) Award offered through the local council. In acknowledging my enthusiasm for Aboriginal studies, my compassion for fellow students and my leadership, I was chosen as the NAIDOC Week Young Achievers Award winner. It was a complete surprise to me and I was very pleased. As part of the award I also received a grant for $500 to use for an Aboriginal education project.

My dad watched the *First Footprints* show on TV and was so impressed he bought the DVD for me to watch as well. We were inspired by this show and thought it should be in all schools as an easy and effective way of teaching Australian students about the original inhabitants of this country, my ancestors. Since then we have received grant money, purchased 18 copies of the DVD, and are distributing them to schools throughout the Campbelltown Council and adjacent areas.

During the last term of the year, we had to do a project on Aboriginal history. We had an Aboriginal Community Education Worker come into our class and talk about the life of Aboriginals prior to white settlement, and then my Dad talked about Aboriginals after white settlement, with a focus on the Stolen Generation. His dad, and his dad's brothers and sister, were taken from their mother when they were young. Both speakers were very interesting. Because I was the only Aboriginal in the class, many of my classmates asked me for help and advice which I was happy to give to them.

I learned so much through the *First Footprints* DVD. The Aborigines of Australia are an incredible race of people, who were not only brave and clever to get here but also to survive more than 40,000 years. Their feats of survival are extraordinary. They were able to live and survive in the harsh deserts of outback Australia, and survived the last ice age more than 20,000 years ago.

Their culture is amazing. Everything important to them is handed down from generation to generation through song, storytelling and rock art. They had no written language. They were the first to produce an image of humans that is now tens of thousands years old. Their art shows much of their history, right through to images that show sailing boats and the first white settlers. I think the most important thing we can learn from their culture is their connection to the land. They look after it as it provides them with everything they need to survive.

It is for these reasons and many more that Aboriginal history needs to be preserved, and I am glad there are many people working to make sure this happens. I would like to see all Australians learn, understand and appreciate Aboriginal culture, so they may come to understand some of the problems faced today by those struggling to do what they think is right to live together in our country.

I would like to continue at Modbury High School where I am now studying, and work with Aboriginal Community Education Workers and teachers to educate my fellow students about our culture. I know that the history of many cultures is taught in schools and they are all important and interesting. However, as we live in Australia, I think a priority should be given to the history of the people of this land.

I hope the students of the 18 schools we have distributed the DVD to get an understanding of how long Aboriginals have been in Australia and appreciate the importance of their culture to Australia's history. I would really like to see this DVD in all schools in Australia, but I don't know how I can do that. I have made a start and maybe with the help of the Aboriginal Community Education Workers, principals, my dad and other Aboriginal organisations, we can get them into more primary schools in Adelaide, South Australia, and maybe even right around Australia.

◇◇

MADDISON DAY *enjoys playing basketball, and would like a career working with animals, maybe even becoming a vet. She is also interested in paramedic work. She likes watching movies; comedies are her favourites.*

A Bolivian journey

TESSA HENWOOD-MITCHELL

My story starts when, as a 17-year-old, I started to appreciate just how lucky I am. I looked outside my backyard and realised that not all children had what I had always taken for granted.

In my final year of high school a friend and I went to South Africa and Kenya and volunteered for two months. I had many expectations and pre-conceived ideas. I was anticipating the Africa I had seen on TV and in the media: the sad, desperate, needy Africa. But what I experienced instead was perhaps the most valuable lesson I have ever learned. I met people who were incredibly resilient, resourceful and appreciative of the smaller things in life. These people were confronted with some of the harshest living conditions I could imagine. However, instead of hopelessness, I saw hope. I realised it is not up to me to 'save' anyone, particularly not people in 'developing' countries. They don't need saving, or rescuing. They don't even need helping. All of those words indicate that they don't have the ability to save, rescue or help themselves.

I came away with the desire to work side-by-side with these communities, to learn from them and to empower them to use what assets they already had to access the opportunities they deserved. I returned to Australia as a passionate and inspired

19-year-old, with no way of turning my passion into anything meaningful. I started studying journalism and international relations at university. However, I was not feeling a connection to journalism as a career option. Changing to social work was one of the best decisions I have made. Suddenly, I was learning things that were meaningful to me.

It was then that I was presented with an opportunity to volunteer overseas as part of my degree. I had been studying Spanish at university. I had also been dreaming of going to South America. I started researching the different countries, and even though I had never really heard about Bolivia, for some reason I knew it was where I wanted to go. It seemed to be such a fascinating place, full of tradition and culture, and beautiful landscapes. It is also considered the poorest large country in South America, with the highest rate of people living below the poverty line.

So I went to Bolivia and spent four months working in an orphanage with around 80 children aged two to 15. However, while I was enjoying my time in Bolivia at my placement, I felt I wasn't doing enough. Being there and caring for the children at the orphanage on a day-to-day basis wasn't going to help them long-term. I felt I needed to do something that would have an impact on their futures and help them find the opportunity to reach their full potential. There were things I was noticing in the orphanage, like no nappies for the babies, no medicine, no running water. Sometimes there was no food. Some of the younger children were behind in their learning. But it wasn't just these specific things I was seeing. I was seeing a lack of opportunity within the whole Bolivian society. There was such passion and such resilience in the population, but there was no support or opportunities for people faced with disadvantage.

I realised I had reached a point where I couldn't in good conscience go back to my comfortable life in Australia and forget what I had seen and experienced without doing something about it. As Australians, the majority of us don't have to worry about where the next meal is coming from, whether our children will have the opportunity to go to school and get an education, whether they will ever be able to get a job, or whether we can afford to visit the doctor for a basic check-up. When it was time for me to come back to Australia, it wasn't an option for me to go back to the same life and do nothing. So I didn't. I came home and within four months, in February 2009, I had set up the foundations of Tia International Aid (TIA). *Tia* is the Spanish word for 'aunty'.

This wasn't an easy process. It was a lot of trial and error, as I created something from nothing, and had to set up everything needed to make TIA a functioning and effective non-profit organisation. Over the last five years we've undertaken some incredible projects with the Bolivian people. These have included nutrition programs for children at an orphanage, replacing a water system at an orphanage to provide clean running water, and a music and computer program for children and young people who are blind. All of our work has the same objective: to create opportunities and enable change for vulnerable and at-risk children and young people.

Our newest and biggest project to date is ValenTIA, which means courage in Spanish. We are working with our local team in Bolivia providing support for young people who have grown up in orphanages, and are transitioning into independent living when they turn 18. When they live in orphanages they are under the care of the government, and their food, clothing, housing and education is paid for. This support stops at 18. Most don't have any family or anywhere to go. Many end up on the streets, unemployed, taking drugs, or getting pregnant early, all because of this lack of support. We're aiming to fill that gap.

There are two phases in Project ValenTIA. The first is a workshop program we are running within orphanages with people aged 14 to 18. It is designed to prepare them to leave the orphanage system, focusing on self-esteem and resilience, values, study skills, health, sexual education and much more.

The second stage is a transition centre for these young people to live and use as a safe place when they leave orphanages. We've started with a place for six young people to live, to trial how it goes. We also have the centre available to any young people who want to receive support as external participants. We offer a number of programs: career guidance; assistance in job searching; education on general rights and responsibilities; managing finances; help with further study (or tutoring to assist them to finish school if they haven't already); a mentoring/big sister program to provide role models; and teaching basic living skills (cooking, cleaning, washing clothes etc.).

We are now looking at opportunities to expand TIA's work into other countries. I can't wait to take what I've learned in Bolivia and look at how I can apply it to working within different communities and cultural contexts.

It hasn't always been easy. There have been moments I've wanted to give up, where I've felt like it's all too much and I'll never be able to make a real difference. I've made many mistakes along the way, and had to learn how to do many things the hard way. There are moments when I wonder what my life would have been like if TIA didn't exist. I've had to make a lot of sacrifices and hard decisions. However, the number of amazing people I've met is mind-blowing, and the opportunities I have been presented with have been incredible. Through all the ups and downs, the one thing that keeps me going is my passion and the knowledge that even if I can just improve things for one person, then I will have lived a worthwhile life.

My biggest piece of advice to people is to act. Don't wait until the day you think you'll be 'ready', or until you know enough or have enough experience. Act now, and don't be afraid of making mistakes.

◇◇

TESSA HENWOOD-MITCHELL *is the founder of TIA, an organisation established in 2009 when Tessa was 21 years old. She completed a double degree of social work and international relations at the University of South Australia in 2013. She currently works as TIA's international director based in Bolivia with the local staff team, overseeing projects and exploring new opportunities for TIA to extend its positive impact.*

A voice for the environment

PETER OWEN

'Never doubt that a small group of thoughtful, committed citizens can change the world. Indeed it is the only thing that ever has ...'
Margaret Mead

I was lucky enough to spend time in my formative years on the edge of the Coorong National Park at the River Murray mouth in South Australia. It's an amazing place – beautiful surf beach and dune system, pelicans, dolphins and sea lions.

In the early 1980s the Murray Mouth closed over with a rapidly expanding irrigation industry extracting more water than the river could sustain. This had a devastating impact on the area and made me realise from an early age the damaging relationship we have with our environment. Advocating for balance between people and the rest of life on Earth has been a fundamental part of my life ever since.

After completing environmental studies and law at the University of Adelaide, I began work at the Conservation Council of South Australia (CCSA) in 2003 to help set up a campaign to restore much needed flows to the River Murray. We distributed information to a broad section of the community and held Parliament House rallies, town hall meetings and media events. With the campaign gaining considerable traction, government funding was cut to CCSA and I learned an early lesson: campaigns for the environment need to be independently funded.

In 2005 I was employed as campaign manager at the Wilderness Society South Australia (TWSSA), an independently funded, community based environment organisation. We launched a number of important campaigns that year, including marine parks and the protection of the iconic Nullarbor Plain. With the health of the environment in rapid decline, there was an urgent need for a system of marine sanctuaries and large wilderness areas on the land.

Unlike the River Murray, the need to protect South Australia's marine environment and remote desert areas like the Nullarbor Plain was not well understood. We decided to focus on education and the coordination of many positive, colourful and artistic mainstream media events. We also worked closely with politicians and decision makers from all political persuasions.

After many years of advocacy, which involved the successful passage of the *Marine Parks Act 2007 (SA)* through parliament and the proclamation of the outer boundaries of nineteen marine parks covering 2,700,000 hectares in 2009, the state government announced the protection of South Australia's most important marine areas in sanctuaries in 2012. This includes the Nuyts Reef, the Isles of St Francis, Pearson Island, areas around Kangaroo Island and the Coorong Coast. It is one of the most significant conservation initiatives in the state's history.

In 2013, again after many years of advocacy and amendments to the *Wilderness Protection Act 1992 (SA)* to recognise the significance of wilderness areas to Aboriginal people, and acknowledge their connection to country and involvement in management, the Nullarbor Wilderness Protection Area was proclaimed. It covers about 900,000 hectares, the same size as the famous Yellowstone National Park in the USA. The spectacular Bunda Cliffs are protected within the area, and when connected to the Great Australian Bight Marine Park, it creates a land and sea conservation estate of global significance.

Major campaigns for the environment generally come up against opposition, with vested interests determined to maintain the status quo. Misinformation may be actively promoted and individuals targeted. Strategies need to be in place to deal with this situation. We decided to ignore it, not to engage in reactive argument and to maintain our proactive positive community message. The strategy ultimately worked, but all campaigns will be different.

To achieve something you have to believe it is possible and recognise that truly worthwhile initiatives take time. Whether the declaration of marine sanctuaries or the protection of the Nullarbor wilderness, the passionate and inspiring staff and volunteers at TWSSA are brave enough to dream and believe in the future.

◇◇

PETER OWEN *is the director of the Wilderness Society in South Australia. He was recently named South Australian of the Year in the Environment Category. He also won the Conservation Council of SA's Jill Hudson Environmental Protection Award in recognition of his role in the protection of vast areas of land and seascape.*

My great big morning teas

MACKENZIE FRANCIS-BROWN

I am 12 years old and have just graduated from my primary school, the Hills Montessori School. I started in the preschool there when I was two-and-a-half years old.

My school is a bit different from most schools. We do lots of community service activities. When we were little it would be doing things in big groups like Water Watch and Clean Up Australia and, as I got older, I could take on more responsibility and work in small groups volunteering within the local community. My school has also been really supportive of anyone who feels strongly about something, so it is not unusual for someone to say, 'I want to do something to help this,' and for the school to find a way to let you do it.

I have held Biggest Morning Teas for the Cancer Council every year since 2005, and have raised a lot of money for cancer research. I also just graduated from the Cancer Council's first Youth Ambassador Project that I have been involved with all year.

I remember when a very close family friend was diagnosed with ovarian cancer. We used to all be in the same playgroup, and her daughter was just a year older than me. Lucinda was three and I was nearly two when her mum died, and I remember that. A few years ago my dad had a skin cancer, but he's all clear now. I know of lots of people who have died or are living with cancer. I want to keep raising money so there can be research to find a cure and people can stop dying. I want to keep doing what I'm doing, but at the same time I wish I didn't need to because that would mean there was a cure.

I really like doing this not only because I can make a difference, but also because it is fun. I remember hearing an ad in the car for the Cancer Council's Biggest Morning Tea. I asked my mum whether I could hold one, and she said we could ask my teacher. It was 2005 and I was nearly four. It was near the anniversary of Lucinda's mum's death, so it must have been on my mind.

When I was little I had a lot of help from my parents to organise the events, but now I do it pretty much on my own with just a little bit of help.

Cancer Council also helps by setting up things you can use to spread your message, like the web page for the Biggest Morning Tea. Since I have used the web page, the message gets out to so many more people, and I raise more money. I can let people know how things are going and they send me messages of support, which is great.

I used to think there weren't very many kids who did this sort of thing, but this year, when I was asked to join the Cancer Council's Youth Ambassador Project, I found there are other kids doing stuff in their own communities. I think that's really cool.

It was great being in the Youth Ambassador Project. We got to go behind the scenes at the Cancer Council and see how the money we raise is spent. They also ran workshops to give us better skills in event management and fundraising ideas.

In the last few years, to get people excited and keen to come to my events, I have come up with different themes. This year was a whole school 'Breakfast in Bed', where everyone came along dressed in their pyjamas (even the teachers) and we had breakfast at school. That was my favourite, especially as there were lots of people and I raised lots of money. I have also organised a 'Mad Hatter's Tea Party', a black and white themed breakfast (where you had to dress and bring food that was all black and white).

Through the Youth Ambassador Project, each person had to complete three challenges: run an awareness campaign, a fundraiser and make a presentation. I ran a campaign about healthy eating, which is one really simple way we can prevent cancer. I made a cookbook of junk food inspired recipes but made healthy versions of them. I gave a presentation at my school where I cooked one of the recipes for everyone to share and gave away the cookbooks.

People have been really supportive in lots of different ways. Sometimes they help me run events, sometimes they help by donating and telling their friends, and sometimes they just say really nice things. All of my friends, family, classmates and teachers are very encouraging.

One of the staff at school (who wasn't even my teacher) nominated me for the Pride of Australia Award. She has had breast cancer and she always comes to the events I run. I didn't win but it was kind that she nominated me.

I remember at this year's Biggest Morning Tea, the mother of one of my classmates, who had cancer, came up at the end and gave me a really big hug and thanked me for what I was doing. She died two weeks before Christmas. It is so sad that her son and husband will have to live with that Christmas memory for the rest of their lives.

I think people who have cancer feel very happy when they

know other people, like me, are out there raising money and that we care. That's why I am going to keep doing what I do, because people are still dying.

◇◇

MACKENZIE FRANCIS-BROWN *has started secondary school at her new school, and has continued her fundraising for the Cancer Council there. She has no idea what she 'wants to be when she's older', but can't wait to see what her future holds. One thing is for sure, she plans to keep on holding Biggest Morning Teas until 'I die or they find a cure for cancer – hopefully the last one happens first'.*

Unfolding projects: Australian and Afghan artists' books

GALI WEISS

There is often a perception that artists are best at creating objects or situations that express a depth of meaning beyond words. The project I'm writing of is about art, words and women, and the interwoven power of all three to create new meanings.

Unfolding Projects began in 2009. At that time there seemed to be an escalation of articles in the media about the dire and desperate situation of women in Afghanistan. They told of women oppressed and persecuted for what the law and people in Australia regard as basic rights. In post-Taliban Afghanistan, a woman can be gang raped and the law does nothing. Her husband can murder her for writing poetry and then go free. Women leaving their homes unaccompanied by a male could be killed. I read of women who defied their families and the law in subversive ways in their struggle to survive mentally and physically.

One central aspect of this struggle was the attempt by women and girls to be literate – simply to learn to read and write. It often resulted in physical persecution; I read accounts of acid thrown on girls and women on their way to school to prevent them acquiring even the most basic education. Such a struggle was in such sharp contrast to my own circumstances and history.

In Australia, I have had the opportunity to study, to develop my intellect, to build up my work skills, to make choices, to aspire. I have been encouraged by the people in my life – my family, my teachers, even the government – to express myself. For me, literacy and art are interconnected.

This is the background to why I was compelled to take some personal responsibility and action, even if seemingly minor, to help women in Afghanistan. It seemed to me that I should do so through what I knew best – my art.

The idea I devised was to create concertina books of images – artists' books – that would be transported in some way to Afghanistan and distributed among women participating in literacy education. Afghan women would be asked to relate to the images within the books by placing text directly in them, in any character or language they desired.

In 2009, I sent an email to a number of Australian women artists, inviting them to participate in a project of dialogue with women in Afghanistan. Thirteen women artists responded positively to the call.

Once I had secured this group, I started searching for a go-between to deliver the artwork. I found SAWA (Support Association for the Women of Afghanistan), a small organisation set up by a group of women activists from Melbourne and rural Victoria. SAWA's convener, Matthias Tomczak, seemed sceptical at first that women faced with daily struggles such as putting food on the table would be interested in an art project. However, we decided to put the idea forward to the women at the Vocational Training Centre for Afghan Women in Kabul that SAWA supports. Latifa Ahmady, the director of the centre, agreed, especially in light of the potential for the project to raise funds for the literacy program.

Each artist in Australia was asked to make a minimum of three concertinas – a total of 53 books were created. Stories by the Afghan women would be written within or alongside the images. The general intent was that the concertina books of images and writing would be transported back to Australia, exhibited to raise public awareness, and possibly sold to raise money. The artistic intent, however, was to take part in a process of support and dialogue with Afghan women who wanted to be literate. It was a manoeuvre that said, 'You are not alone.'

At our first artists' meeting before the concertinas were created, questions were raised by the artists: How do we know what interests Afghan women? How do we know what women in Afghanistan relate to? How do we find a common theme? The answers were very clearly: We don't. That was not our concern, just as we would not expect the Afghan women to write what they thought we would want to hear.

The aim was not so much to find a common theme, as to present ourselves through what interests us, in keeping with our individual arts practice or expression, and by doing so, to 'meet' with the other as we are. In other words, to present ourselves through our images, in our difference, even at the expense of mutual understanding, and finding common ground with the women in Afghanistan through the use of the artists' book as a space in which to meet and express ourselves. We had to be prepared that we would never see the books again, or that the Afghan women students would reject the whole idea. In our discussions the artists came to an agreement: each concertina was a gift, a gesture, an offer. Once the gift was given the artwork was no longer in our hands nor in our control.

By April 2010, 53 artists' books by 14 women artists (including myself) from various parts of Australia were personally delivered by Matthias to the Vocational Training Centre for Afghan Women, together with a letter of explanation and writing tools from the artists. Latifa was enthusiastic about participating in the project, and began to interest the students immediately after Matthias's departure. Nevertheless, for some time, we heard nothing.

After months of silence in which it seemed the project may be faltering, Matthias inquired gently by email. Latifa explained the reality of the women's situation: their absence from school during the Holiday of Eid, followed by the turmoil of the 2010 elections which resulted in casualties for some of the students, teachers and their families. Despite all this, as she had indicated previously, the women were still interested and she would ask them to work on the books in their homes as well as at the school. Two weeks later, Latifa emailed digital photographs of the concertinas with writing – the first visual evidence of contact between the artists and the writers.

In November 2010, just over six months from their delivery to Afghanistan, 36 books returned by airmail to Australia. Each one was marked with handwritten text, at times on ruled pencilled lines, at times overlapping the images, or placed around them. The return of each book to Australia imbued it with meaning; the material had travelled a great distance, within a particular period of time, and that bore witness with its marks. It returned familiar but changed. It was both the space of, and record of, human interaction.

The use of the artists' book and printmaking in this project is not only about the capacity of these art forms to distribute information to a wide audience, but about humanizing a situation in multiple ways. The books have the potential to involve us – participants and viewers – in a way that the media, or even social media, cannot or has stopped doing. While this project does not assume a political stance by denouncing a political or social situation, it does enter a political sphere through a choice of action, no matter how seemingly minor.

As Barbara Kameniar, SAWA's Melbourne representative at that time, has noted, the sharing of marks on paper is a political act with a political intent; it says, 'Afghan women be strong, we are with you. We are women too. We stand in solidarity with you. We choose to act with you in our hearts and minds. You are not forgotten.'

In 2012, the State Library of Queensland acquired the books for inclusion in its artists' books collection, one of the largest public collections of artists' books in Australia. In 2013, SAWA and the artists self-published *Two Trees*,‡ a book that documents the project and includes essays, images and stories from all involved. All proceeds from sales of *Two Trees* are passed on to the Vocational Center for Afghan Women in Afghanistan.

Finally, I will end with the words of Latifa Ahmady from her essay for *Two Trees*:

> Afghan Women are beaten. They are confronted with several violences, put on fire or stoned. They are in search of a minute to relax and breathe. Presenting a gift or award, even asking about their living condition is just like a dream for them. So under such conditions the support of Australian women and the sharing of their ideas with them is the greatest gift in their lives.

---

‡ *Two Trees: Australian Artists' Books in Afghanistan and Back*, eds Gali Weiss, Barbara Kameniar & Matthias Tomczak, Fremantle, WA, 2013

The gift has evolved into a mutual exchange, and has resonated with the public in ways we could not have envisioned at the project's beginnings.

GALI WEISS *is a Melbourne-based artist with an extensive record of exhibitions and projects. She holds a PhD from Victoria University, 2009. Gali is represented in the National Gallery of Australia and the state libraries of Victoria and Queensland, and is currently a lecturer in Creative Practice, Deakin University, Melbourne.*

If the River Murray Mouth could speak

DIANE BELL

I am an anthropologist. It is the prism through which I analyse the world and the ethical framework within which I act. I like doing fieldwork where I live. I like the accountability.

The work I have chosen to do is with groups at the margins, with people whose voices are muted, ignored and scorned. My most recent work on 'environmental matters' may look like a shift from my earlier feminist anthropological work but it isn't. It is more social justice advocacy and activism. My questions destabilise the established order. My persistence violates the politics of politeness. Speaking truth to power does not bring accolades. I continue to do it because

- it matters,
- I have the knowledge,
- I care deeply about the country, my fellow citizens and the land on which we live,
- I have seen the consequences of not speaking, of forgetting, of silencing – and
- I think our democracy is in crisis.

On my return to Australia in 2005, after 17 years in the US, I chose to settle in Ngarrindjeri country, near the Murray Mouth in South Australia. It is a part of Australia that is dear to me from my work with the Ngarrindjeri who fought to save their sacred places over the Hindmarsh Island Bridge affair. During this shameful episode in Australian legal-politico life, the Ngarrindjeri's stories were recognised, then challenged. They were found to be liars, but later vindicated. They received an apology and their site was registered, but the damage had been done. We need to do better. We need to learn to listen to the stories of the land, respect the country and act accordingly.

River Stories

As anthropologists we spend a great deal of time listening to how people tell their stories; matching what they do with what they say; testing rhetoric against reality; and distilling key cultural symbols and articulating core structures – social, economic, political, gender, religious, artistic, legal. I've been listening to River Stories – hotly contested stories concerning how to address the devastating 'Millennium Drought' of 2000–2009 across the Murray-Darling Basin. The land was ailing. Communities were stressed. The Ngarrindjeri foretold the crisis. Their stories offer context and critique for the crisis, and gesture to a healthy future.

A staple Ngarrindjeri story concerns two fishermen who, having filled their canoe with big fat fish called *Thukeri*, are approached by a stranger who asks, 'Hey brothers, I'm hungry. Have you got any fish to share?' They say, 'No, we haven't got many fish. We only have enough to feed our families.' So the stranger began to walk away. Then he turned and said, 'You have plenty of fish and because you are greedy and don't want to share, you will not enjoy the *Thukeri* fish ever again.' When the fishermen unloaded the fish they discovered they were bony. The stranger, they later learned, was *Ngurundjeri*, the major creative hero and lawmaker of the region.

We might think of this story as a cautionary tale about over-allocation, of the impact on the broader society of individuals taking more than they need. The Murray-Darling Basin was the food bowl for Indigenous people for many millennia before settlers regulated and over-allocated the waters. Their story prompts us to ask, 'What are we growing, for whom and why?' Years of mismanagement brought us to Code Catastrophic, but do we have a vision of an integrated future for this dry continent? In what kind of society do we want to believe? How do population targets, foreign affairs, models of economic development, our rivers and water policies connect? And they do connect. The River Murray will continue to teeter on the brink if we cannot respond with integrity and act with purpose.

In listening to River Stories during the 'drought', it seemed to me that two opposing clusters of narratives were driving the political agenda. On one hand I heard the confidence exuded in techno-fixes and market economics. 'We can engineer our way out of the crisis.' 'The market will solve the problem.' These stories assume rivers can be 'managed'. Their imperative is to dam and disconnect. The economy is privileged over the social and when it fails the profits are privatised and the losses socialised. On the other hand, narratives were struggling to be heard. Scientific studies were grounded in longitudinal data; Indigenous cautionary tales were attuned to the rhythm of the land. These were stories of connectivity, interdependence and relationality, honoured in the breach rather than observance.

Water as a 'thing' generates different policy responses from a river as a 'living body'. Water-as-thing asserts rights in and control over the commodity. River-as-body evokes responsibilities, an ethic of care, stewardship for the future, and respect for a powerful living force. Until there is conceptual clarity on this point I think the life of the river will be brokered against the rights asserted by 'users' of water. The cacophonous calls for 'balance' by stakeholders with competing interests will continue to drown out the life world of the River. Many voices. Many stories. And where in all this was the voice of the River? I see creating a space for this voice to be heard as a necessary step toward action; by articulating the competing stories, exploring their genesis and, in so doing, laying bare the incommensurability of the worldviews that underpin the narratives.

From story to action

Where? How? To me it was obvious that action was needed at the local, state, national and international levels. This entailed alliances, local action groups, petitions, submissions, delegations, letters to editors, op-ed pieces, surveys, newsletters and flyers.

At the local level we organised with great determination and creativity. As an incorporated local action group, we entered into a *Kungun Ngarrindjeri Yunnan* Agreement (Listen to Ngarrindjeri Speaking) with the Ngarrindjeri, wherein we recognised their ownership of the country and they stood with us in the struggle. We created a new institution, the Fresh Water Embassy, evoking the Aboriginal Tent Embassy of 1972. Our embassy spoke for the species that were being silenced. Our website logged our actions and attracted visitors from some 56 countries. We were everywhere: community meetings; Senate inquiries; out in the wetlands with a pH metre. We held educational forums, planted the foreshores, violated exclusion zones. We petitioned, protested and prodded our elected officials. We sang our way through our Murray Christmas Song Book on the steps of Parliament House in Adelaide; the media called it the most unusual carols they had heard. You have to have some fun. Before the state and federal elections of 2010, we succeeded in getting all parties to fill in a questionnaire on the Murray–Darling and published the results.

We were instrumental in stopping the weir that would have dammed the Murray at the point where it flowed into Lake Alexandrina. The two million tonnes of salt that come down the river system each year need to be flushed out through the lakes and the narrow Murray Mouth to the Southern Ocean, not stuck behind a weir and banking up the system like a cancer. It was a very bad idea. We made a scale model of the proposed weir. The planners had not bothered. The minister would not look at it, turned her back. We took the model on the road and it had its own blog. The techno-fixers moved further downstream to Clayton Bay, where the River Murray picks up fresh water from Currency Creek and Finniss River, and put in a 'regulator'. We kept a peaceful vigil at the site and staged a wake for the River when the regulator dammed its journey to the Mouth.

During the so-called drought, it was clear there was fresh water in the system. There was water for sale. It could have been purchased on the open market. Courage and vision would have been needed to get it through the system and out the Murray Mouth. Instead a risk-adverse state chose a quick fix. The Ngarrindjeri joined with Indigenous nations along the Murray-Darling on a 2300-kilometre pilgrimage to the Mouth, as they sang the spirit back into the River and themselves. The floods came. The flush occurred. Some of the blockages were removed, slowly and with poor grace.

The Murray Mouth Manifesto

Manifestos are public declarations of principles and intentions, often political in nature. The word derives from the Latin *manifestum*, meaning clear or conspicuous. That is what is needed: a clear and conspicuous rallying point. The Murray Mouth is now open. What would it say if it could speak? Here is my draft for the Murray Mouth Manifesto:

> A spectre is haunting Australia – the spectre of privatisation. No longer do we share a vision of the just society, rather we seek profit. We have to grow, grow, grow. The economy must be fed. More rice, more cotton, more cheap wine.
>
> - There is legislation to protect me and bring my lifeline and all who depend upon it back to health, but the Murray-Darling Basin Plan is deaf to the science.
> - There was $10 billion to be spent on going from a history of failure and mismanagement to a new relationship with me, but rather than buy back the water for me, you have appeased stakeholders with more infrastructure.
> - Your 'experts' have measured, modelled and maddened me, and then brokered the results in the name of 'balance of interests'.
> - You survived the Global Financial Crisis. Well done. Now for the Global Environmental Crisis. I have reached 'peak water'.
>
> What story will you tell?

◇◇

DIANE BELL, *award-winning author, anthropologist, river advocate, attempted retirement, but the Murray–Darling River crisis could not be ignored. She ran as an Independent (2008 Mayo State by-election), then continued the environmental fight with speeches, press releases, blogging and unlikely lyrics. She has been published widely and is professor emerita of anthropology, George Washington University of USA, and writer and editor in residence, Flinders University, South Australia. She currently lives in Canberra.*

An Indigenous prime minister in our lifetime

ANDREW PENFOLD

Like a lot of people, I knew about Indigenous disadvantage long before I understood it. Growing up in inner Sydney, I saw how it affected the lives of some of the kids with whom I used to spend my days. I saw it, but I didn't understand it, because I didn't understand the impact of my own choices at the time.

My father died when I was six, so my mum worked long hours, late nights and weekends to support me and my sister. I had a lot of freedom and I spent my life knocking around the streets with local kids from Sydney's Glebe and Redfern. By the time I reached high school I had stopped paying attention, and sometimes I didn't even bother to show up.

When I was 15, my mother and grandmother intervened, convincing St Joseph's College, Hunters Hill, to take me in as a boarder. At the time it was the last thing I wanted – I felt all my freedom was being taken away. I was quite happy with my life as a rebellious teenager. But it wasn't long before I stopped fighting and started working. I went from bottom of the class in Year 9 to topping the class in Year 12 in mathematics, history and economics.

Boarding school offered structure, boundaries, discipline, role models and good teachers. I was forced to do homework, go to bed early and eat three healthy meals a day. There was a lot of mateship and sport, which kept me active, engaged and tired.

The four years I spent at boarding school changed my life. I went on to study law at university and, over the next two decades, worked for some of the biggest international firms in Sydney, London and Hong Kong as a lawyer and an investment banker.

My education wasn't a gift, although the opportunity was. I earned my education because I worked hard. Nobody gave it to me. My education was an opportunity and, without it, the life I've lived would not have been possible.

My experiences up to this point taught me the value of a quality education and all that goes into it: great teachers, supportive networks and a stable environment. I saw how it opened doors for me and how the lack of an education closed doors for others, Indigenous Australians in particular. I had developed an understanding, but it wasn't until I suffered a personal tragedy that I was inspired to act.

In 2002, I was living and working in Hong Kong with my wife Michelle and our two daughters (our son was born in 2003). On Saturdays I played rugby with a close group of friends. That year I missed the team trip to Bali and I was at home in Australia with my family when twelve of my mates were killed in the bombing of the Sari Club.

Faced with this devastating loss, I teamed up with a couple of mates and drew on my experience in law and banking to establish a charitable fund, the Hong Kong Rugby Bali Fund. We ended up raising several million dollars, distributing the funds to the widows and orphans of the team, as well as supporting the education of around 100 Balinese children whose parents had been killed or injured in the blast.

The project carried me through my grief and left me feeling

inspired and empowered. More importantly, it showed me that I could use my skills to make a difference to people's lives.

Soon after, in Sydney, I heard my former school had started enrolling a small number of Indigenous boys. I was intrigued so I arranged to meet the headmaster. I was so inspired by what he told me that I offered to raise several million dollars in order for the Indigenous program to grow and continue to serve as an example for other schools.

In 2004 I retired and moved back to Sydney. I spent the next five years working full time, pro bono, to establish the seven-million-dollar St Joseph's College Indigenous Fund, which currently helps to support up to 40 Indigenous boys in perpetuity at the school.

The success of the Fund inspired me and my wife to work with schools around Australia. In 2008, working from a makeshift office in our dining room, we established the Australian Indigenous Education Foundation (AIEF) with a single scholarship. In 2015, AIEF is offering over 500 scholarships at 35 partner schools and colleges in NSW, Queensland, Victoria and Western Australia, as well as universities across the country.

AIEF's mission is to empower Indigenous children to build a brighter future for themselves and for the nation.

In 2008, we set out to raise $40 million to help educate 2000 Indigenous children at leading Australian schools and universities, and support their transition into meaningful careers. Over the past six years we have raised more than double that amount – $85 million – through partnerships with the Australian Government, leading corporations and charitable foundations. Buoyed by this success, in early 2013 we increased our funding target to $140 million and now aim to support 7000 Indigenous students over two decades.

This funding supports two core programs: the AIEF Scholarship Program, which provides scholarships at schools and tertiary residential colleges, and the AIEF Pathways Program, which assists AIEF scholarship students to develop the personal skills necessary for the transition from school to a successful career.

Our model is low cost, scalable and sustainable. We work with hard heads, soft hearts and capable hands, and we are setting the benchmark in good governance and transparent and evidence-based reporting, while producing tangible results.

At more than 90 per cent, AIEF's retention and Year 12 completion rate is the highest of any federally-funded program in Australia, and almost 100 per cent of students in the AIEF program have embarked on a productive career pathway after completing secondary school.

It is universally accepted that education is the biggest barrier to Indigenous equality in Australia. AIEF does not have all the answers to this problem, but we do have one that has been proven to work. We don't believe our scholarships are for everyone, but we believe that Indigenous families who want these kinds of opportunities should be able to access them, irrespective of their personal circumstances.

We look forward to the day when organisations like AIEF are no longer needed. In the meantime, we are committed to educating Indigenous students – the majority of whom are being let down by the education system today.

In early 2013, AIEF commissioned a Newspoll survey, which revealed two thirds of Australians did not expect to live to see an Indigenous prime minister. With almost all of our alumni pursuing productive careers, and with almost half at university, we hope we can change that.

ANDREW PENFOLD AM *is the CEO of the Australian Indigenous Education Foundation (AIEF) and a member of the Prime Minister's Indigenous Advisory Council. In 2013 he received the inaugural NSW Human Rights Award, becoming the NSW Human Rights Ambassador, and the Chancellor's Award for Excellence from the University of Technology, Sydney. In 2014 Andrew was appointed a Member of the Order of Australia for significant service to the Indigenous community.*

Life's unrecognised moral mentors

LORNA HALLAHAN

Moral mentors. I have been blessed by many in my life. And most of them considered not really respectable.

When I was 16 I was diagnosed with bone cancer, underwent a leg amputation, and then submitted myself to two years of chemotherapy and rehabilitation. I guess I had been (since the dawning of an adolescent consciousness of a world beyond family, school and church) a political progressive. In class and dinner table discussions, I had supported action against the damming of Lake Pedder, the withdrawal of Australian troops from Vietnam, and Aboriginal land rights. Being compelled to leave this everyday world, and reside for several months in a congregate rehabilitation centre with people whose lives were not showing any of the positive direction that mine would take, really sharpened my sense of justice and compassion. I learnt about the meanness of those charged with the care of dependent people. I learned about the fear and the rebellion of the cared-for; and what it takes to hang onto dignity in a world that sweeps you aside. I left vowing that I would never forget these people. Once it looked as though I might not die, I set a new life goal to become a social worker because that was the closest profession I could find that linked values, knowledge and action.

It was a good choice. Social work opened many doors for me as I tried to live out my vow, and to live in ways that would not contribute to the unnecessary suffering of those who rely on the rest of us to build a better world. I have never had a job titled 'social worker', and most have been poorly paid. However, it is more than 30 years since I graduated, and I have never been without employment or purpose. I have worked in an international student Christian organisation with a focus on human rights, in the anti-uranium and peace movements, with youth organisations, and for an ALP politician. I have worked, paid and unpaid, since the late 1980s, within the independent living and disability rights movement with an enduring concern for those who cannot defend their own rights and construct their own wellbeing.

Best of all has been the ongoing learning from all the people who are part of that vibrant stream of history – the fellow activists, the fellow 'cripples', the families of those who believe you don't have to live indecently because you have an intellectual disability, Aboriginal storytellers, and people labelled as 'mad'. They have been family members, friends, clients, co-workers and enemies. The struggles and gutsy action of these people showed me a way to live that was big, hopeful, generous – even transcendent. And demanding. Not one of these people will ever be recognised with big pay packets, awards, honorary degrees or glowing speeches.

I grew up in a family making that familiar transition from working to middle-class and, sadly, my new friends and comrades were not always welcomed as worthy. Yet they seem much more truthful and caring than those who were presented as the very model of virtue. I discovered that virtue often has more to do with what's in your heart than what's in your pants!

During the mid 1980s, I worked with the only female member of the Labor Opposition in Queensland. From her, and a gay Anglican priest who supported me in my early days as an organiser, I learned just how important it is to be able to get close to people who would never count in any elite. To respectfully visit and converse with; to relish stories of prized children; and to acknowledge confessions of weakness. To accept help. To work out ways they can contribute to our movement. And to laugh until we wept. We regularly reflected on whether we sought social change because we had experienced marginalisation – he gay, she black, me disabled – or because we had an informed vision of what might make things better and some ideas about how to go about it. We never really resolved this tension, but we kept going wherever the opportunities opened up. And every one of those tiny, but often opportunities taught me more about how to be an activist.

People skills are core to being a good social worker/organiser. Early, I learned how to work out which meeting I needed to be at and which I could avoid; to design posters and stick them up in the dead of night. I realised I could use all those analytical and group work skills I learned studying social work to get the most from meetings. To work out whom I needed to convince of the merits of my planned action. To know my place and bide my time. It taught me the skills of working collectively.

Later, when I finally connected with the small but energetic disability movement, organising became harder and I had to get more serious. Here I had to deal with my own identity. Does privilege make me less of a disabled person? We know that the overwhelming experience of disability is one of rights denial, threat and actual violence, poverty, exclusion and loneliness. This is not my life. Does my brief and traumatising immersion in the disability service world provide me with grounds for enduring solidarity with those who will never know the social acceptance and care which is part of my everyday life?

I have given up the sham of invincibility that surviving teenage cancer offered me. (The Freudians will have fun with that one!) I realised I had to lose my grandiosity and arrogance to engage in 'forthright thinking' about disability. I had to ask, observe and think to really understand what it means to align with people who are widely believed to be better off dead. I had to tell of their oppression by those who are saluted for their righteousness. I had to honour the exhausted efforts of those who say 'no' to the lie that disabled people have no place among us. And to deal tenderly with those who believe the shit they get is all they can expect. To help them see that their lives can be comfortable, filled with love and acceptance, and rich in every way; that welfare dependency is not as impressive as a supported life in the community of your choice. Sadly, this is never the political goal.

The most amazing moments are here with these people, experiencing their generosity, compassion and acceptance. At these points, resentment is pushed away and a vision of loving justice seems possible. That is the role of a true moral mentor. To keep us believing that, as Alice Walker puts it, 'we can share this Earth as unashamed friends'.

So being an activist is about using my skills to work with people. About being able to honestly, and without self-deceit, see how oppression thrives in places badged as caring. About opening myself to ongoing education by those whose lives need freedom and justice, in order to live morally and compassionately. And, therefore, to challenge a smug community with confidence, to see that in hiding those who challenge our view of a worthy fellow human, we hide vital parts of ourselves that we need to liberate if we are to ever share our plenty with all.

◇◇

LORNA HALLAHAN *is associate professor and head of social work at Flinders University, where she is also chair of the Social and Behavioural Research Ethics Committee. She has been involved in the disability movement for 30 years, and has recently been active in policy advice roles including as chair of the South Australian Ministerial Disability Council, deputy chair National People with Disability and Carers Council, and member of the National Disability Insurance Scheme National Advisory Committee.*

The business of sex work

DEBORAH McCULLOCH

Rebecca West wrote that she was called a feminist only when she said something that distinguished her 'from a doormat', or, she added, 'a prostitute'. The activist project I did in the 1980s and persist with today is about sex work. It aims to decriminalise it; it should be conducted as a business similar to physiotherapy, massage, tattooing, or counselling.

When I discovered feminism I was a lecturer in English at a teachers' college. I was also discovering sociology and at university had read Gunnar Myrdal's works about women and African Americans in US life. I became obsessed by the low wages women receive for their work, the sex segregation of that work in Australia, and the way women's education trained us for our subordinate positions. And these facts of life are still true. Over our lives, women who work full-time earn 20 per cent less than men. Women who are single parents are often paid barely enough to cover the expenses of a child, have to live in poor housing near poor schools, and struggle with poverty all their lives – for themselves and their children.

As I listened to women's stories at conferences, in small groups, among friends and at work as a femocrat, as South Australia's first Women's Adviser to then premier Don Dunstan,

I became more distressed by the rape and domestic violence women suffer. When many women talked about our society, and how it permitted these crimes or promoted them, they also named pornography and prostitution as examples.

I don't think I have ever met a porn star, but I met several sex workers. Don Dunstan was such a wonderful premier because he understood the process and power of legislation so well. In my first year on the job he had criminalised rape in marriage, a bold step. Don said he had to answer questions about it from San Francisco to Munich. What needed to change with sex work? The workers said the law. I said we could change that, but Don disagreed. I thought he was wrong, but experience has proven he knew better.

In 1980, SA parliamentarian Robin Millhouse introduced a Bill to decriminalise sex work but it was defeated within the year. I was no longer employed in the public service so was free to research whatever I liked, and for some years I worked closely with sex workers – all women. I got to know Stormy Summers and Sylvia Glennon, the president of the Prostitutes Association. These women and others allowed me and other non-sex workers to share something of their knowledge and practice.

First of all they were not cowed. They were not timorous or quiet, or held in a spell by men. On the contrary, they were strong women with a thorough understanding of the ways the law defeated recognition of themselves and the work they do. Second, it is work, and its purpose is money. While many women I met enjoyed the work, they became involved because of the money. One woman told me that after her husband had abandoned her and their two sons, and she had found them somewhere to live, she had enough money for a tin of baked beans. 'What choice did I have?' she asked. 'My kids come first.' Third, they were impatient with the condescending and ignorant views of their work held by many.

The same attitudes cropped up again and again:

- The men, the clients, were invisible. Nobody discussed them. Nobody asked who they were, when they were not being clients. Nobody researched them. If people started to ask about them, someone changed the subject.
- In much that was said, a woman who arranged the service was held responsible for it. If a crime had been committed, it was by her. In our laws, dating from the 1950s, nowhere did it say that working as a 'prostitute' was illegal. But only the women were prosecuted for breaking regulations or the laws that surrounded sex work – like 'living off the earnings'. Theoretically, one's children are guilty of this absurd and demeaning law. What other occupation lives with this level of control from outside forces?
- The women were considered to be helpless, utterly vulnerable to any demand of the client. In fact, one woman who became a sex worker said she had never heard or seen a loud or angry word or act from any client in a brothel. Ever. She argued that a brothel is women's territory; men know this and behave in an exemplary fashion. And these women have been dealing with men for years; they know how to control behaviour. To assume they were helpless victims was to disparage their knowledge and skills.
- The problem was the law not the practice. The SA law assumed it had a role in the matter. Over the 15 years or so when parliamentarians such as Ian Gilfillan, Carolyn Pickles and Sandra Kanck tried to decriminalise sex work, references to 'a common prostitute' or a 'common bawdy house' had been removed from the *Criminal Law*

Consolidation Act. But the *Summary Offences Act* remained and still remains. Part five sections 25–26 deal with soliciting, procuring and living on the earnings. And part six sections 27–32 with brothels.

- When feminists listened to sex workers, we found that changing the law was the most important thing that could be done. Under the law, the police could enter any premises, harass workers and the owners of buildings, set traps to establish that a person was a sex worker, and constantly shake the industry. The definition of 'a brothel' was a problem: a brothel is a place where an act of prostitution occurs. With this definition, any sex worker was vulnerable to police interference, despite an act of commercial sex not being illegal.

So we talked and wrote and explored the ideas of sex work and the law. In the 1980s, Professor Marcia Neave was employed to conduct research and recommend how sex work could be decriminalised. Bills were presented, but MPs lost their nerve. SA is the only state in Australia still operating from laws written in the 1950s.

SA parliamentarian Stephanie Key introduced a new Bill, one that would not only eradicate the eight sections in the *Summary Offences Act*, but also extend to sex workers the same rights as other workers, such as including them in the *Equal Opportunity Act* and WorkCover. The Bill was defeated in the SA Parliament by one vote in November 2013. Stephanie redrafted her Bill and reintroduced it, but there was not enough time to debate it before SA elections were held in March 2014.

Steph's background in workers' rights brings a new level to the debate: feminists have claimed our rights to control our own bodies, and Steph recognised the assumption that sex workers could be denied human and industrial rights. Her Bill is a real advance in the arguments for women and for workers. Look what a good MP can do!

◇◇

DEBORAH McCULLOCH AM *discovered feminism while a lecturer in English at a teachers' college. She subsequently was a leading figure in the South Australian Women's Movement, as co-founder of the Women's Electoral Lobby (WEL) and the first Women's Adviser to an SA premier – Don Dunstan. She has been a long-standing advocate for the need to decriminalise sex work.*

Politics at the end of life

JULIA ANAF

As a postwar baby boomer, my early years were shaped by a political landscape transitioning out of the Menzies era, and into a time of great change signified by the United States civil rights movement, and the momentum of early second wave feminism. My first experience of activism was joining an anti-Vietnam War march, followed over the years by other street marches or rallies in support of issues including women's rights, gay rights and animal welfare. The impetus was always a mixture of anger, impatience, a growing understanding that change would never happen without grassroots activism, and the excitement of being part of the groundswell. These sentiments came to the fore again when, by chance, I became involved in the voluntary euthanasia law reform movement in the mid-1990s.

Struck by a perceived tension between two separate issues gaining prominence at that time, I was writing a thesis on the 'politics' at the end of life. One issue was a growing concern over Australia's rapidly ageing society, and the associated 'burden of care' that had invited a sensationalist subtext that *non*-voluntary euthanasia may be on the longer-term political agenda for economic reasons. The other issue was the growing international social movement advocating the right to choose voluntary euthanasia in the face of unremitting suffering from a hopeless or terminal illness. This was an issue that had not been addressed as part of wide-ranging social reforms in South Australia during the 1970s, including decriminalising homosexuality and legalising abortion. The growing push to legalise voluntary euthanasia was underpinned by the argument for liberty, but was strongly resisted by the state. I was interviewing the late Mary Gallnor, former president of the South Australian Voluntary Euthanasia Society (SAVES), to inform aspects of my thesis, when she persuaded me to join the society, giving me the same assurance that she had been given: 'You won't have to do much.'

SAVES formed in 1983 as an initiative of the Humanist Society of SA, based on values of compassion and social justice, with law reform the primary aim. In time I joined the committee, a small team including founding members of the society. SAVES had already developed a range of publications including the handbook 'The Right to Choose', was engaging in political lobbying and with the broader community, and had begun a dialogue with the Australian Medical Association. As part of wider community engagement, SAVES had drafted an anticipatory direction or 'living will', was responding to distress calls from members of the public, and had provided input into ethics courses in medical schools.

Over time I found myself focusing more and more on this one issue, reflecting on why it had become a priority when there were so many other important causes. I found it difficult to determine how much the driving motivation was a wish to be part of the excitement of this growing international, national and state movement, or my own need to deal with the guilt that comes from 'averting ones' eyes' from what seemed to be a resolvable problem. The motivation was probably both, underpinned by the ongoing reality of what professor of sociology Allan Kellehear refers to as 'shameful deaths', racked with pain and indignity. I could accept, sadly, that many forms of physical and emotional suffering cannot always be relieved, but found no credible reason why futile suffering at the end of life could not be circumvented within the context of a sound and overarching legal framework. After all, the only thing needed was political will, as supporting a person's right to die under his or her own conception of dignity would make no real demands on the public purse. Somehow this made it seem even more unjust.

It brought to mind Iris Marion Young's contention that emancipatory politics involves conceptions of domination and oppression that stem not only from *material* injustice and inequity. In addition, I recognised having legal recourse to voluntary euthanasia is an issue that may well affect us all personally, through our familial ties and loved ones, or from just knowing that someone, somewhere, is experiencing suffering that can only be relieved through the assisted death he or she is denied. I felt a growing anger at what I perceived to be powerful vested interests representing a small minority thwarting law reform by cowing elected MPs. This was the injustice of maintaining the status quo that was challenged by medical ethicist Dr Brian Stoffell. As he put it, 'Cruelty is the principal vice and institutional cruelty is worse than odd cruel episodes. Laws that cause cruelty by perpetuating unwanted and unnecessary anguish, pain, humiliation, degradation and fear must be swept away.'

I was motivated to become more active but felt some trepidation in joining a team of people from a diverse range of professional backgrounds who seemed comfortable being in the spotlight. I understood that fear can be a real barrier to action, but also realised that most people do not become activists by disposition; nor do they have any formal training. Nevertheless a tension persisted between wanting to play a part, but needing to find the right 'patch' in the organisation and having the security of a bounded role. While I was not fearful of 'putting myself on the line', or standing up for what I believed in, I understood my character was more suited to a behind the scenes or support role. I also felt that I could contribute more through the written word than I ever could from a public podium or as a spokesperson for the media. While I have always admired and envied people who could go head-to-head on the debating stage with a 'silver-tongued' opponent, I instinctively knew that this would never be me. However, would my need for such self-imposed role limitations preclude me from being a 'real' activist?

SAVES' committee was well rounded, having recruited a range of volunteers with a mix of complementary skills: financial, computing and information technology, political (gained from party affiliations and understanding parliamentary processes), counselling, and writing and editing. I found there was room for both frontline and backroom players in SAVES as in other activist groups. In 1999 I took on the role of editor of the *VE Bulletin*, and helped compile some of SAVES' many fact sheets and publications. I began writing numerous letters to newspapers and seemed to achieve a high publication rate, wrote occasional articles for other publications, and assisted in sending letters to MPs to keep them informed of important developments here and overseas. This would be my contribution toward keeping the issue of voluntary euthanasia law reform on the public agenda, and also the means by which misrepresentations made by some opponents of change could be addressed.

Each committee member took on her or his dedicated role

as well as the shared roles, which still include staffing stalls on Awareness Days held regularly in Rundle Mall, having a regular SAVES presence on Parliament House steps, assisting at public meetings and attending rallies. In earlier days SAVES members were in demand as speakers to community groups, but due to growing awareness and widespread acceptance of the issue this demand has now waned. 'Life' issues are contentious as they reflect sincerely held but polarised positions, so I had to be prepared for the occasional negative responses that came in the form of letters-in-reply to my letters in the press and through personal correspondence. It was interesting to get occasional anonymous letters successfully delivered by Australia Post addressed to just my name and suburb in response to a letter in the *Advertiser,* South Australia's daily newspaper.

Activists thrive on hope but must be prepared for disappointment. There has been a Voluntary Euthanasia Bill before parliament every year since 1995 with only a narrow window of opportunity before it eventually lapses, or before politicians become nervous about the status of the electoral cycle. We see how members of parliament who are prepared to put up a private member's Bill are constrained by the limited time available for debate. Therefore, when we heard a Bill was about to come to a vote in the upper house in November 2011, there was the excitement of a 'mad scramble' to get to Parliament House to observe proceedings and to support the politician who may well have been about to make history. It failed by a small margin and we were there, by that time well after midnight, to commiserate and support each other following long and tense proceedings. The mixed emotions of being so close but realising there was still a long path ahead made us even more convinced to keep on trying.

When we begin to feel defeated, such as in this instance, we reflect on the commitment of the suffragettes who, a century ago, became more militant in their long fight, engaging in hunger strikes and chaining themselves to railings; experiencing many legislative defeats before finally achieving success.

◇◇

JULIA ANAF *is a research associate of the Southgate Institute for Health, Society and Equity based at Flinders University in SA. Her current research interest is the impact of the practices of transnational corporations on health. She is vice-president of the South Australian Voluntary Euthanasia Society (SAVES).*

Building peace through social justice

ANDREW ALCOCK

Xanana Gusmão, the first president of East Timor, was asked by Australian journalists in 2001 if he supported George W. Bush's War on Terror. He said the attack on New York's World Trade Center could not be resolved by having another war. He thought it was much more appropriate to use international law to bring the perpetrators to justice. He knew full well that many innocent people would die tragically. The events in Iraq and Afghanistan have proved him correct. He went on to say that we could only build world peace by pursuing the politics of international social justice and love.

Many people, from Xanana Gusmão to my parents, have had an impact on my life and led me to believe that, where possible, I should do what I can to make a difference to advance human rights, social justice and environmental responsibility. Their examples have inspired me through a lifetime of activism including working for an independent East Timor and West Papua.

My parents, for example, had a big impact on my early thinking about social justice and human rights. Gwen, my mother, was a fundamentalist Christian, and my father Alick was an atheist. They were both originally quite conservative politically. Gwen was a very generous person and used to go out of her way to help others. As a trained nurse, she was able to help neighbours when they were sick but anxious about doctors' fees. I have come to observe her nursing help of others as 'Gwen's Triage Service'.

Alick, a worker in a butter factory for most of his life, taught me to think widely. He was a keen admirer of Mahatma Gandhi because of his great contribution to the winning of India's independence and his attempts to rid the country of its caste system. Like my mother, he was prepared to help community organisations and ordinary people when practical jobs needed to be done. In the final ten years of his working life, Alick was a painter and decorator. He took a Robin Hood attitude to his charging of fees – poorer people paid very little and the wealthier paid more.

Largely because of my mother, I was sent to the local Methodist Sunday school. In the Bible class we discussed war and peace, social justice, Aboriginal rights and socially responsible use of money.

At an early age, I became concerned that so many people had their human rights violated or faced persecution, did not have enough to eat or were not adequately clothed, lacked adequate shelter for their families, and found it difficult to educate their children.

I was later to discover that during the Industrial Revolution of the 18th century, the Methodist chapels that sprang up in Wales and Cornwall became the birthplaces of many of the unions in Britain because of their work to feed the poor and provide some medical services to workers and their families.

I was very much influenced by people supporting the Student Christian Movement (SCM), a world movement that started in

1898, and a group of which I was a member during my high school and university days. It took a very open approach to Christian teachings and throughout its history promoted social justice and peace. It always promoted dialogue with members of other religions and philosophies including Marxism. Although it was originally Protestant, it did much to promote ecumenism and helped establish the World Council of Churches and the Uniting Church in Australia.

Another person who had a great impact on my thinking was Geoff Harcourt, a former economics professor at Adelaide University and, later, economics reader at Cambridge. Geoff was Jewish and lived in the Jewish community in Melbourne. As there were no Jewish schools when he was young, he was sent to Wesley College. While there, he was exposed to much racism from his fellow students, which made his life unbearable. A key person who helped him at Melbourne University was both a Methodist theologian and a socialist.

Geoff told me that as he became a Christian, he also became a socialist. He was very active in SCM and the Campaign for Peace in Vietnam. In those days, university life was rather conservative and formal, and Geoff was one of the few academics who had a very egalitarian approach toward his students. Apart from being involved in the peace movement of the day, he was involved in the left of the ALP. He encouraged me to read about the US war in Vietnam and this led to me getting involved in the peace movement against that war and to think about joining the Communist Party of Australia (CPA).

During a visit to the Philippines in 1975, I met Father Hector Maury, an Italian Jesuit priest who supported liberation theology and was the founder of the National Sugar Workers Federation of the Philippines. It may seem strange, but when I told him friends had asked me to join the CPA, he embraced me and urged me to do so.

My 15 years in the original CPA were inspiring. I discovered a group of people who were dedicated to social justice, human rights, equal rights for all, and protection of the environment at home and abroad. The CPA did so much to give support to many activists in the progressive social movements in this country.

There are others who have inspired me: leaders of the liberation theology movement who have done so much to change lives for the better in developing countries; priests I met in the Philippines and East Timor; refugees from Latin America; those involved in the resistance to Nazism and fascism during the Second World War and since; and those involved in struggles for liberation, such as Nelson Mandela, Xanana Gusmão, Aung San Suu Kyi, Salvador Allende, and many Aboriginal leaders in Australia.

I am not a religious person these days, but I know my ethical framework comes largely out of Christian, Buddhist and Marxist thinking. I do believe in a socialist type of spirituality that links the people who want a world where everyone has enough of the world's resources to live well, where human rights, social justice, equality and environmental sustainability are top priorities. There are many who are prepared to exploit other people and the environment to make huge profits. Fortunately, there are also many others who fight for human decency, equality and freedom.

APHEDA (Australian People for Health, Education and Development Abroad) has the motto 'Help to Make Life Fair Everywhere'. To me, this sums up what the life of a true activist should be about.

ANDREW ALCOCK *Andy's paid and unpaid work has traversed many fields: high school teaching (including two years as Australian Volunteer teacher in Malaysia), union organiser, OH&S Officer, Australia East Timor Friendship Association (SA), international solidarity and peace activist, and environmental health and human rights activist. He believes in a socialism that has a respect for human rights and the Earth's environment and continues a longstanding involvement in justice issues in East Timor and West Papua. In August 2014, he was awarded an Ordem de Timor-Leste – Medalha (the Medal of the Order of Timor-Leste) by the Timor-Leste president, Taur Maran Ruak.*

A life-changing disease motivates and inspires

ELIZA BARTLETT

At nine years of age my life dramatically changed when I was diagnosed with type 1 diabetes. Despite being told I had to live the rest of my life on multiple daily injections, and having to monitor my blood sugar levels with finger pinpricks five times a day, I was never going to let this diagnosis stand in my way. It was never going to be an excuse or a barrier; instead it motivates and inspires my actions.

I instantly received sympathy from everyone, and still do to this day. I don't want people to feel sorry for me, so instead I try to prove being a 'diabetic' does not hold my life back. Despite saying this, type 1 diabetes is a life-changing and dangerous condition, and there is certainly nothing more I would like in this world than a cure. I have not only experienced the lows of the disease, but have seen them firsthand in patients. As a recently graduated registered nurse, I have seen the crippling effects, such as heart disease, blindness, kidney disease, nerve damage, limb amputation, plus many more, due to the complications of diabetes.

In April 2013, I walked from Adelaide to Melbourne, just under 800 kilometres, to raise money and awareness for type 1 diabetes. Being young, healthy, and with a real passion for the cause, I knew I could make a difference, and that nothing was going to stand in my way.

It took me a gruelling 20 days, walking around 11 hours and 40 kilometres a day. I encountered some of the most difficult challenges in my life. By day two I started to get severe blisters, which worsened each day, and required medical treatment. Due to the lack of medical facilities, I had to wait to day six to get to a hospital in Keith. By the time I made it, the blisters were covering my feet and needed debridement, antibiotics to treat infection, and sterile dressings. I had expected to get blisters, but blisters such as those could have resulted in complications and amputation of the feet, as diabetes leads to poor circulation of the extremities.

As early as day four, the real injuries began. I had damaged multiple tendons, and had stress fractures in my feet and shins. At times my feet would completely give way from under me. Mentally, I was still tough and motivated, and nothing was going to stop me getting to the Melbourne Cricket Ground to finish my journey. At this stage, one of the most difficult things was overcoming the people around me who insisted I had no choice but to stop.

The emotional journey was one of the most unexpected challenges I faced. I have never been a very emotional person, but with each step I took a new feeling surfaced. Being alone, on a very lacklustre road, I had plenty of time to think about and reflect on what I was doing.

The support I received on the journey was incredible to say the least. The way the public rallied behind me honestly eased the pain and kept me going. It also helped me realise I was creating the awareness of type 1 diabetes I had set out to. Each donation I received, and each message sent, meant more to me than I could possibly express. I was sent letters from families affected by the disease, had cars stopping on the side of the road, and people I had never met going out of their way to donate and send me messages of support. It was also great to have the support of high profile people in the community. I had the likes of Shane Crawford, ex-Australian Rules footballer who had previously covered the same route on foot, calling, messaging and tweeting constant support. I also had current and past Australian and international cricketers, current AFL footballers, and members of both national and community media teams following my journey.

I began my walk at Adelaide Oval with the support of the South Australian Cricket Association, as two members of the South Australian Redbacks walked with me to the outskirts of Adelaide. As planned, I completed my walk prior to the Adelaide Crows versus Carlton AFL match at the Melbourne Cricket Ground. I had the chance to attend the pre-game lunch of the Adelaide Crows, and visit the Carlton dressing rooms before walking onto the ground. Their help in reaching the broader community was significant.

The support I received allowed me to pass my goals, and raise over $25,000 for the Juvenile Diabetes Research Foundation (JDRF), while achieving greater awareness in the community. My main aim was to promote awareness and dispel the common misconceptions about the differences between type 1 and type 2 diabetes. While there are minor similarities, type 2 diabetes is a preventable and manageable disease, compared to type 1 diabetes, which is an autoimmune condition with no cure, and can affect anyone regardless of their lifestyle.

My first thought upon finishing the walk was, What's next? I am planning another journey in 2015 and considering travelling across the USA. In the meantime, I am completing a diploma in diabetes education and management, with career goals of becoming a diabetes nurse educator. I want to help other people living with diabetes, and prevent the disease from burdening them, instead allowing them to live a full and productive life like me.

◇◇

ELIZA BARTLETT *was a finalist in the Young Leader category of the Pride of Australia Award 2013. She continues to raise funds for the Juvenile Diabetes Research Foundation and plans to work as a diabetes nurse educator in the future.*

Corporate dominance versus democracy

SHIRLEY COLLINS

My story began in 2008. Working at the computer late one night, I clicked on a video file I had not yet viewed. It had a name that told nothing of its contents. Strangely, there was only audio, no picture. From the darkness came the earnest, impassioned voice of a young girl, about the same age as my son. Speaking directly to me as if my own child, the voice was urgent.

> You adults must change your ways. ... I am fighting for my future ... for all the generations to come. ... I am only a child, and I don't have all the solutions, but I want you to realise, neither do you! ... If you don't know how to fix it, please stop breaking it! ... At school, even in kindergarten, you teach us how to behave in the world. You teach us not to fight with others, to work things out, to respect others, to clean up our mess, not to hurt other creatures, to share and not be greedy. Then why do you go out and do the things you tell us not to do?... My Dad always says, you are what you do, not what you say. Well, what you do makes me cry at night. You grownups say you love us. But I challenge you, please make your actions reflect your words.

It was a plea I could not ignore. I had to act, and now. But what could I do? Caring for the environment and people were the key messages I heard. So that night I joined the Greens for the environment, and Amnesty International for the people, and the story unfolds from there.

The young girl was 12-year-old Severn Cullis-Suzuki, speaking for the Environmental Children's Organization (ECO) at the UN Earth Summit in Rio de Janeiro in 1992. Her message is as relevant today as then, even more so. We don't know how to fix the holes in our ozone layer. We don't know how to bring the salmon back up a dead stream. We don't know how to bring back an animal now extinct. And we can't bring back the forests that once grew where there is now desert.

That same year, Western Australia held a state election and the government changed from Labor to a Liberal–National coalition. Almost immediately, the new Barnett government moved to lift two statewide moratoriums on uranium mining and genetically modified (GM) crops. Why? What had changed? Had the reasons for the moratoriums been resolved? I had been working full-time for years to give my family a good quality life, but I was seeing tomorrow's world for my children was being ransomed and destroyed before they'd get there. I followed the debates as they progressed through the WA parliament. I heard politicians from all sides arguing caution: to apply the precautionary principle because of the risks of chemical pollution, and genetic damage we don't know how to fix. I saw politicians whose actions did not reflect their words, who should have crossed the floor to vote but did not, who chose short-sightedness and the party line over their children's future and their conscience. With the numbers stacked against us in both houses of parliament, the moratorium on uranium mining was lifted and exemptions passed to allow two GM crops, Bt cotton and Roundup Ready canola, to be grown in WA.

This should have been headline news. I expected the debates to be blazing in mainstream media. But it was quiet. Why?

So began my discovery of corporate dominance versus democracy. Investigative journalism is critical to democracy, playing a key role in holding powerful interests to account. If the media won't tell the story, we have to do it ourselves. Before writing my first letter, I had to research the issues thoroughly: searching the internet, social media and campaign groups; attending seminars, presentations, study tours and field days; and buying and borrowing books and DVDs. I soon realised that I could never research everything, but I could learn who to trust and be guided by them.

On uranium mining and nuclear power, my early mentors were Dr Helen Caldicott, documentary filmmaker David Bradbury, and Greens senators Jo Vallentine and Scott Ludlam. To keep me on track, I watched the video *Chernobyl Heart*, read about radiation refugees in Irene Zabytko's novel *The Sky Unwashed*, and looked for news updates on the Fukushima Daiichi Nuclear Power Plant disaster in Japan.

On genetically modified organisms (GMOs), my early mentors were the Canadian geneticist and environmentalist, Dr David Suzuki (yes, Severn's father), and the Italian Carlo Petrini who, in opposition to Fast Food, founded the international Slow Food movement on the principle of food that is 'good, clean and fair'. I soon became aware that GMOs were driven by multinational chemical corporations with links to pharmaceutical companies. This is described well in the French-Canadian documentary *The Idiot Cycle*.

The 'Big Six' chemical companies are Monsanto, DuPont, Syngenta, Bayer, Dow and BASF. They are buying up seed companies around the world. You can also add Pacific Seeds, Pioneer, Sumitomo and Nufarm. Monsanto is the dominant player and owns most of the gene patents on GMO seeds.

Although Monsanto was ranked by Covalence EthicalQuote as the least ethical multinational company in the world, the WA Government sold it a significant share of the public wheat and barley plant breeding company InterGrain, to develop GM wheat and GM barley despite worldwide market rejection. With CropLife as the industry lobby group and at odds with action on climate change, they are perpetuating chemical-addicted, fossil-fuel dependent industrial farming, with growing control over the world's food supply. This trend is extremely concerning, given the strong correlation with increasing health problems such as allergies, asthma, obesity, diabetes, autism, depression and cancers, especially in children.

My mentors today are independent scientists, lawyers, farmers, chefs, NGOs and campaigners who care about sound science, responsible implementation of new technology, seed freedom, food sovereignty, agroecology, biodiversity and, to quote wholefood chef Jude Blereau, food that can 'heal, nourish and delight'.

In 2013, it was rewarding to be one of the local organisers of the worldwide March Against Monsanto in Perth, rallying for our farmers, our food and our future. On 25 May and 12 October, millions of people marched in events around the globe, in six continents, over 50 countries, 400 cities and in every state of Australia. It is encouraging that the people of Hawaii, Vermont and elsewhere are starting to have some legislative wins against the chemical/GM corporations. Artists and musicians add exceptional insights, enjoyment and inspiration. Notably, rock legend Neil Young released his 36th studio album in mid-2015 titled *The Monsanto Years.*

A farmer-to-farmer court case over GM contamination was recently heard in the Supreme Court of Western Australia. Marsh v Baxter is a landmark case, although there have been many GM contamination incidents around the world from Monsanto's patented GM crops. In the US, Monsanto has, on average, sued one farmer a month for royalties. Many countries have banned GM crops, while others from time to time reject shipments or embargo imports of grain or honey at risk of GM contamination.

In Australia, the GM industry has dismissed contamination incidents as 'adventitious'. However, when contamination from a neighbour's windblown GM canola caused most of Steve Marsh's organic farm at Kojonup, WA to be decertified, his only recourse for loss of his livelihood was common law. The judgment on 28 May 2014 dismissed the case, finding in favour of the GM farmer. When allowing GM canola to be grown, no legislation was put in place to deal appropriately with the inevitable contamination events. This was an unprecedented test case that failed at the first jump, proving that common law is inadequate, despite the Government's assurances. It has reignited the community's call for proper legislation and regulation to protect GM-free choices of farmers and consumers. In September 2015 the Court of Appeal again ruled in favour of the GM farmer in a two-to-one decision, with the President finding in favour of Steve Marsh. He is now seeking special leave to appeal to the High Court.

With the Australian Greens, the GM-Free Australia Alliance, the Australian Food Sovereignty Alliance, the Safe Food Foundation and many wonderful others, we will continue to campaign for appropriate laws and regulations for comprehensive labelling of GM food and feed, to allow GM-free farmers to farm without threat of GM contamination, and to preserve the integrity of organic food.

In closing, I would like to pay respect to Argentine neuro-scientist Professor Andrés Carrasco who died on 10 May

2014 aged 67. His groundbreaking research on the effects of glyphosate and Roundup on embryos is challenging regulators to re-examine the safety and use of these chemicals. The world has too few independent scientists. He will be sadly missed.

◇◇

SHIRLEY COLLINS *combines a background in mathematics, education and information technology with a keen interest in citizen science to speak up for the environment and people. She is a passionate advocate for family farming, resilient rural communities and a food system that is good, clean and fair. Shirley lives in WA.*

From peak oil to our own garden

MICHAEL DWYER

My education in peak oil began when I attended a meeting in Adelaide where Michael Lardelli spoke about the world oil supply. He pointed out how oil discoveries no longer match usage, so obviously delivery of diesel and petrol in Australia is going to decrease sometime in the future.

He launched a final fact I didn't absorb until after the meeting. Nearly all our food relies on fossil fuels thanks in part to the kind services of the dinosaurs who, 150 million years ago, helped manufacture our cheap and abundant oil. No oil means no diesel to run machinery to fertilize, plant, irrigate and harvest crops, and to transport the produce to the supermarket. No oil means no food.

The cars streamed past me as I cycled home. My thoughts were disturbing me deep down. What if the drivers couldn't afford petrol? What if petrol ran short and the price rose to $4.50 a litre? What jobs would exist at that price? What if the food didn't get delivered to the supermarket, what if, what if ... but the politicians don't see a problem so it must be all right.

I began to search the internet. I read how the pros and cons were argued out in peer-reviewed scientific studies, philosophical thoughts and emotional rants. There must be hundreds or even thousands of intelligent people who have thought long and hard about oil supply, substitute fuels, economics, geology, fracking, you name it. After much thinking and backtracking, I reached my own conclusion and a sinking feeling built in my stomach. The world has a problem.

Never mind the rest of the world, I have a problem! What about my job, my mortgage, my super and all our plans and dreams for the future? How will my wife and the kids get by in a world when the easy times fade away? My Peak Oil Blues is documented as a grief-like process where the sufferer goes through stages of denial (they got it all wrong), anger (why do those politicians keep us in the dark?), depression and finally, acceptance. Following acceptance comes the decision to DO SOMETHING.

Some days later, Michael Lardelli suggested we form a group. We needed a name. Adelaide Peak Oil was no good. It's not the lead up to when the maximum rate of petroleum is extracted which requires action; it's organising what to do afterwards in the declining resource-poor future. The name became Beyond Oil South Australia (BOSA). We decided we would raise the issue with the media and politicians, and try to affect public policy.

We managed to hold a few small demonstrations in Adelaide's city centre I am sure no one remembers. We got our spots on radio and succeeded in getting a few articles in the Adelaide *Advertiser*. We did letter-drops and called public meetings few people attended. We sponsored overseas speakers. We created a newsletter list of hundreds of interested people. Was it all in vain? Who knows. Many people have heard of peak oil now, but most don't understand the full implications declining energy supplies will have directly on our way of life and civilisation.

But we raised awareness and it was fun mixing with like-minded people. That's the key. Once you discover something that needs to be done, find like-minded souls who want to do it too.

Over the years I learnt about transition. Finally someone has a plan to move away from the economists' preposterous myth of perpetual economic growth. One of the BOSA people, Graham Brookman, was way ahead of me. He understood the food puzzle since the early 1970s; how the so-called 'Green Revolution' was simply a faster way of exploiting fossil fuels to produce food. My wife and I attended the week-long Permaculture Design Course at the Brookmans' Food Forest. I was a little concerned we would be mixing with faded hippies or left wing zealots but it was nothing of the sort. We learnt, we discussed, we ate great food and more importantly we connected with one another. There are a lot of small active groups of all hues in Adelaide.

'Think global, act local' is one of the expressions in the sustainable world community. Know the big picture but do something local – anything, no matter how small, because democratic politics in a consumer society is incapable of tackling such a confronting issue as the end of our way of life. It will be the grassroots movements that find the new way, supported of course by nature, which will knock us about something fierce with climate change fires, climate change storms, floods and relentless resource shortages. Besides, doing something positive feels good; it makes the Peak Oil Blues irrelevant.

We did guerrilla gardening in the Adelaide Parklands and planted some fruit trees. Then I met others through the local council who wanted to create a community garden in the beach suburb where I live. It is never easy working with councils; they have a hundred conflicting issues to contend with. The first attempt at starting the garden was unsuccessful. But it raised the idea in the local area so that four years later, armed with a federal grant, the council encouraged me to help start the Glenelg North

Community Garden. It is now thriving and we are having lots of fun and making many friends.

Where to from here? The world is not standing still. World population pressures, compounded by declining resources and climate change, are causing famine, terrorism and resource wars. In Australia, the consumer has not yet understood the pressures now in play, and we still have undying faith in perpetual economic growth. Most of us know we will never travel to another planet, and yet most of us ignore the clear evidence of permanent peaks in the world supplies of oil, fish, water, arable land and phosphate.

And Adelaide? Life will become hard, but as Malcolm Fraser quoted: 'Life wasn't meant to be easy, my child, but take courage: it can be delightful!'

When you discover something important and it's worth doing, pursue it and find like-minded people to work and play with. Our community garden will, over time, turn into a focus where many local people will learn how to grow their own food and look after their own chooks in the backyard. And it will all be worthwhile.

◇◇◇

MICHAEL DWYER *is an instigator of the Glenelg North Community Garden, co-founder of Beyond Oil South Australia, and a cyclist who rode from Perth to Adelaide and is now one of the lycra-clad, fast bicycle set. He is an amateur writer and member of the SA Writers' Centre. He thinks food is very important and loves cooking and conviviality.*

MADGE takes on the GM industry

FRAN MURRELL

MADGE stands for Mothers Are Demystifying Genetic Engineering, as well as Mothers Advocating Deliciously Good Eating.

MADGE started in 2007 when the Victorian Government decided to review the genetically modified (GM) canola moratorium that was set to expire in February 2008. Glenda Lindsay, Jessica Harrison and I decided to set it up and used the name MADGE from the New Zealand group, Mothers Against Genetic Engineering. They had folded before we started, but had made a striking poster of a naked woman on all fours with four breasts linked up to a milking machine to highlight the direction GM was taking agriculture.

Glenda and I met a few years previously through Bob Phelps from Gene Ethics and had worked on GM campaigns, including making seed and food mandalas.

I'd never heard of Jessica, but I got home one day to find a message on my answer machine from her suggesting we all dress up as cows and do a demo outside the United Dairyfarmers of Victoria (UDV), calling on them to maintain their opposition to GM canola feed. The UDV had been instrumental in the 2003

Victorian GM canola ban coming into effect. I had no idea who Jessica was – Bob suggested she ring me – but I loved her style. So Glenda, Jessica and I did a press release, organised a rally dressed in cow suits, and MADGE was born. Amazingly, others came and one farmer, dressed in a cow suit, had a friend take a photo that was published in her local paper.

We were having a coffee after our efforts, while still in costume, when we heard the UDV had supported feeding GM canola to cows. I grew very angry. I believe people should know what is happening to their food. GM companies, like Monsanto, should not be able to change the fundamentals of what we eat without our knowledge and consent. We started the MADGE website and digest to let people know and decide for themselves if they want to eat GM. Facebook and Twitter came later.

Eight years after MADGE began we still have unlabelled, untested GM food in the supermarkets, but many things have changed. There are farmers' markets, community gardens, guerrilla gardening, school kitchen gardens – as well as groups like the GM-Free Australia Alliance and the Australian Food Sovereignty Alliance. These groups, and others, link people locally, nationally and globally.

The food movement is on every continent and those who are part of it are incredibly diverse. They believe that food produced in a delicious, fair and healthy way is intimately linked to justice and respect for people and the Earth. So many of the problems we face, including poverty and climate change, can be significantly reduced by looking after the people, plants, animals, water and earth that nourish us. My work with MADGE has brought me many friends and wonderful experiences, and a richer way of being in the world.

FRAN MURRELL *learned about GM crops when her first child was a year old. The promises of reduced pesticide use made GM crops sound attractive but the more she investigated the more concerned she became. In 2007 she co-founded MADGE Australia Inc, a group of mothers and others trying to sort through the spin on GM food. She has spoken on this topic nationally and internationally.*

Save the Duck Pond

M. ISABEL STORER

I remember returning to Adelaide shortly before the attractive Foy and Gibson building at the corner of Rundle and Pulteney streets in Adelaide was demolished to 'put up a parking lot'. I was bemoaning its demolition to one of the guests at a party and he asked me what I had done to protest. When I replied, 'Nothing,' he said, 'Neither did anyone else. It would have needed only one protest for a reassessment to have been made.'

In the 1960s I woke one morning to hear chainsaws and went out into the street to see council workers about to cut down centuries-old gum trees. I asked them who had given permission and as they prevaricated I told them to stop. They did.

Like the three little pigs, the next morning they were at work even earlier.

The third morning they asked me to leave them to cut the trees as I 'probably had housework and washing to do at home'.

Naturally that annoyed me. I contacted various government departments to check and discovered that permission had not been given for the secret felling activity. The work was stopped.

Those trees stand to this day and I pass them thinking of the man who slipped the council workers a few dollars to cut them down so that gum leaves would not fall on his lawn. This was the beginning of my life as an activist.

I married young and had four sons. As a family we travelled widely, living in various countries for three to six months, at times with little knowledge of the language or culture of our host country. I suppose this sort of life experience helps one to cope with difficulties and challenges.

When I saw what I considered to be an inappropriate and expensive proposal for a new 'statement' entrance to Belair National Park, I was compelled to protest.

The proposed entrance involved major works, the building of bridges over creeks and a road up a steep slope. Part of the plan would turn Playford Lake, traditionally a tranquil area for contemplation, bird viewing and quiet walks, into a giant roundabout. The ambiance of the area would be destroyed. The existing entrance could be modified to achieve a similar solution with regard to traffic flow, the stated reason for changing the entrance.

I approached a local MP who more or less said, 'Go away. You are probably the only one who does not think this a good idea.' I met with the Head Park Ranger who felt sure that I would like the idea if he met me on site and showed me the proposal. We met on site and discussed the planned changes.

It was distressing to see that two large gum trees, planted over a hundred years before as part of an avenue along one of the older entrance roads, had already been felled. Even as we met, people stopped to ask who was responsible for cutting the trees, calling their removal an act of vandalism.

Although many good changes were proposed for the park, it seemed that the ambiance of the area had been ignored. It was important that it be maintained. The money could be used more wisely. I went about ensuring that information about the proposed changes was brought to the attention of the public and local residents, and users of the park in particular.

It was time to enlist more help. I spoke with friends and neighbours. I spoke to the local press, radio stations and TV news channels. Always keen for a story, they were happy to give the issue publicity. Photos were taken of the lake, reminding the public of the privilege of having access to such a beautiful area so close to the centre of the city. Radio stations gave air time and groundswell grew. Television coverage increased the public's awareness of the details of the proposal.

Many people offered to help. Local schools and kindergartens used the area for environmental experiences. I spoke with these groups and they took up the baton. Letters were sent to MPs and the Council mayor joined the fight along with a district community group.

One of the local MPs was willing to help by printing flyers for a public meeting to resolve the issue. A date was set. 'Save Playford Lake' became 'Save the Duck Pond' – a title that didn't please the purists but caught the attention of the public. More articles appeared in the local press and we got further coverage on radio and TV. A local school provided a venue and I coordinated a group to help hand out leaflets at the park. Others helped me letterbox the area adjacent to the park.

My family continued to support me, and my son ensured that on the night of the meeting the sound system would work. We expected maybe a group of 100. People kept pouring in to the meeting hall. We ran out of chairs and standing room. Local people were the predominant group, but there was also wide support from various groups across the city and suburbs. It was obvious from the outset that the 400 or so people did not want the entrance to go ahead as had been planned. They preferred maintaining the tranquillity of the area. Even MPs who had previously not shown support turned up, and switched to my side when they saw the mood of the meeting.

By the next morning, it was once again 'back to the drawing board'. It was arranged that the local mayor, the works manager, the minister and myself would meet at the park to discuss the contested proposal. The minister halted any further work.

A small committee consisting of the mayor, the chair of the local residents group and me met and assessed alternative proposals. Eventually we had a final meeting on site where several alternatives were offered, some reasonable, some not. A practical change was agreed upon that ticked all the boxes.

I was amused when the new entrance was opened. History had already blurred. The person who officiated told me how prudent the minister had been in selecting the design. The local mayor interrupted, saying it had actually not been her decision, but had come as a result of my intervention.

The Duck Pond, Playford Lake, remains tranquil, its ambiance continuing to attract visitors.

◇◇

M. ISABEL STORER *continues her activism with lobbying, although mainly written protests and lately via Letters to the Editor. They must make some sense, she says, as many have been published. She is currently battling with the city council over the need for the continued maintenance of paved footpaths. The preservation of the Adelaide City Park Lands is another area of interest. She has also recently been involved in drawing attention to the role the Ann Flinders Club played in the early days of Flinders University.*

Ordinary people can change the world

CHRIS LOORHAM

I grew up in suburban middle-class Melbourne and was educated in Catholic schools. My mother was the most significant early political influence in my life. She was forced into the workforce to support my sister and me following the death of our father at an early age. She says that being the breadwinner of the family caused her to question many of the conservative middle-class political attitudes of the 1960s. Voting Labor for the first time was, for her, a revolutionary act, if not a mortal sin. She was a great reader and we would often discuss the political and historic books she was reading at the kitchen table. When I was a young teenager she taught me to question the values of our social class.

Politics was also discussed at St Bede's College Mentone where I was exposed to a different set of values. The Vietnam War was the defining political issue of the day. And I enthusiastically joined the debate with other students from more typically conservative Catholic homes. I was usually in a minority of one. Some of the debates were quite heated with me being labelled the school communist. I remember one student shouting at me, 'Better dead than red!' and looking like he meant it. Such were the political tensions caused by the Vietnam War among the Catholic community. I retaliated by scratching 'Ho Chi Minh' into my desk and wrote an article for the school paper on student dissent. I never felt the need to rebel against the school. To the credit of the De La Salle brothers in charge they did not attempt to silence me; notwithstanding a delegation of parents who visited the headmaster in an attempt to rid the school of communist influence.

It was through this debate that I gained the confidence to express my beliefs in a hostile environment. I remember standing on my own, handing out anti-war leaflets on the steps of our parish church one Sunday morning after mass.

The environment I entered at Monash in 1970 was anything but hostile to leftist views and I enthusiastically devoured the full smorgasbord of left ideology on offer. I always felt socially privileged and never had a personal need to revolt against the establishment as such, so the extreme left politics of many students never appealed. Most of these students went on to take highly paid corporate positions following graduation.

Most of my activism was focused among my fellow law students where some of us were able to move the Law Students' Society to some sort of social relevance. We organised a campaign against various rip-off merchants and succeeded in getting pyramid selling outlawed. Law students actually picketed an unethical auction house in Swanston Street and succeeded in closing it down. Ralph Nader, a US consumer advocate, was visiting Australia and a few of us at Monash helped organise his lecture tour. I was attracted to his model of student activism, based on using the intellectual resources of university students to research the facts in order to disseminate the truth about consumer or environmental concerns. We used this model to establish the Public Interest Research Group at Monash, which conducted a number of research projects into environmental and public health issues. The particular project I was involved with was an examination of environmental problems in the Dandenong Ranges. We got together a team of eight students, raised the funds to pay ourselves $50 a week to research the issues over our vacation, and published a report with recommendations. We were mainly undergraduate pass students. Our report was awarded a Robin Boyd prize for Environmental Design by the Royal Australian Institute of Architects, and a group of ordinary students became the experts on the future of the Dandenong Ranges. Our recommendations were taken up by the local residents and largely implemented by the state government. This taught me that ordinary people could change the world.

In parallel to my political activism I have always felt a deep interest in nature. Had it not been for my interest in environment law, I doubt I would have completed my law degree. Following the success of the Dandenong Ranges project, I was offered the position of legal advisor to the Commonwealth Government inquiry into sand mining on Fraser Island in 1975. This was my first legal job. Following months of hearings, an inspection of the island and painstaking research, the recommendations of the inquiry were accepted by the conservative government of the day and there has been no mining of mineral sands above high water mark on the island since.

Had it not been for John Sinclair, in many ways a very normal man, and a small band of local supporters, sand mining would be all over the island today. During the campaign John, who was the leader of the local scout troop, led his scouts onto the parade ground at the Maryborough Show to be booed by the local miners and their redneck supporters.

I vividly remember standing under a majestic rain forest canopy beside the crystal clear waters of Eli Creek on Fraser

Island with the presiding Commissioner, Dr Hookey, when he asked, 'Where are we now, Chris old boy?' I replied, 'We are on Mining Lease ML 523, John.' He paused. 'And how are they going to rehabilitate this?' he said. In the end the future of the island all came down to that simple question.

I then worked for a number of years as a criminal lawyer, including working for the Aboriginal Legal Service in Victoria and Alice Springs. My most satisfying work was to represent the Aboriginal Community groups who were trying to restrict the availability of take-away alcohol in central Australia. By building united fronts with the non-indigenous community, including church groups and the NT police, notorious take-away licences were closed down and others refused permission to operate. This had a marked impact on crime rates. Despite the withdrawal of government funding supporting this initiative, Aboriginal people pressed on regardless and mustered broad support for their campaign. I have been told that being Aboriginal in this country is to be a political activist 24/7.

In 1992, I took on the role as Principal Solicitor with the Victorian Environment Defenders Office (EDO) at a time when it had run out of public funding. Through the support of sympathetic barristers and solicitors working for some of Melbourne's major property law firms, the EDO was able to grow during these lean years and successfully launched its first prosecutions and planning appeals to defend the environment on behalf of ordinary people. My work at the EDO taught me that support for change can sometimes come from unexpected places.

We are living in a different world from the one where I gained my activist experience. Going to university now is like being on a different planet compared to when I was at Monash in the early 70s. I still believe it is ordinary people who can change the world.

In general I am cynical of parliamentary politics and wonder why perfectly sound environmentalists spend so much of their energy involved in that cesspool. I believe that our power as consumers to protect the Earth is yet to be tapped by the environmental movement.

◇◇

CHRIS LOORHAM *is a planner who has a background in legal services. He has worked as Principal Solicitor for the Environmental Defenders Office, and with the National Native Title Tribunal. He now works as a planning consultant and mediator based in Port Fairy, Victoria.*

A brush with peace

JUDY BLYTH

I'll start my story in 1986 when our family moved from Melbourne to Perth. Already a member of People for Nuclear Disarmament (PND) in Victoria, I quickly rejoined in Western Australia. The Palm Sunday Peace Rally was imminent. I turned up in PND's Hay Street office just as final preparations had been upset by the discovery of plans by a Young Liberals group to muscle in at the head of the march with a banner declaring PEACE THROUGH STRENGTH. I suggested that PND paint a banner declaring its diametrically opposite view on the matter and simply ensure that it got in first. This was greeted by a wail about the lack of time available to produce such a banner. I'd made banners for Friends of the Earth when I'd coordinated its Eltham branch for five years and I thought I could manage. That was how I came to produce a banner proclaiming SECURITY THROUGH PEACE that was carried behind PND's main identifying banner. After this, the job of banners just stuck to me.

Somehow my calico painting expanded – and I became a sort of banner 'go to' person for many social change organisations. Why not, when I had all the tools needed: a sewing machine, a collection of oil painting brushes inherited from my maternal grandmother, and even a gardening smock from a beloved aunt on my father's side. All this gave me a sense of connection with my forebears as I acted as a conduit toward the future world these various groups sought. I could see that their many issues were linked, each relating to how we humans treat one another or the environment; how awareness and empathy with one issue flowed into others through the activism expressed by those I met. Banners became a tool for finding these wonderful people and learning about their thoughts and connections. It felt good and right to have a paintbrush in my hand.

Designing banners was fun and often done literally on the back of an envelope that had good proportions for the job. I learnt to make bold eye-catching designs in bright colours with a short and pithy message. One of the challenges was achieving this necessary brevity, but in time I improved. Of course, those asking for banners were helpful and frequently I would receive explicit directions.

One of the highlights came when I was asked to paint a banner to accompany the public event in Perth where Prime Minister Kevin Rudd made his Apology to the First People of this land. The large tent housing the huge television screen was crammed and the many-hued crowd spread way beyond it. The emotion in the air was overwhelming and tears of joy were shed. It was the best thing Rudd did as prime minister. Whenever I paint I feel part of the issue, and it was beautiful to share in the powerful feelings that day on the Esplanade by the Swan River.

Having been keen on better management of our waste, I was entranced with South Australia's *Beverage Container Act 1975*, which became operational in 1977 when our two kids were in primary school. I worked on the issue with Friends of the Earth in Victoria, longing to see the day when other states would follow that five-cent deposit and refund scheme for drink containers, ensuring that most were recycled rather than dumped in landfill. I picked up the issue again in WA when Senator Scott Ludlam was pushing for a national scheme. The Greens were doing great work on it, clearly presenting the need and means for implementation. So was the Conservation Council of WA and I befriended a dynamo called Mika Leandro who was coordinating its campaign for a ten cents refund scheme. We did much together – and, of course, banners were involved, as well as other props including painting two gloriously bulging pregnant tummies whose inhabitants demanded a Cash for Cans solution to littered beaches.

Now I've six wonderful grandchildren and even one great-grandson, but a national drink container refund scheme or even one in WA still eludes us. Hats off though to the Northern Territory for facing down the big packaging and drink industry (especially CocaCola Amatil) and implementing Cash for Cans there.

For about ten years (until 2005), I worked as WA branch office staff for Medical Association for Prevention of War (MAPW). As well as engaging with this group of inspiring and thoughtful doctors at monthly meetings and national conferences, I did my best to produce their newsletters, and draft submissions on defence and disarmament matters and write letters presenting their comprehensive views to the media. There were, of course, banners to be made, such as on the campaign for a global ban on landmines. On MAPW's behalf, I participated in meetings in the office of the Christian Centre for Social Action where a group coordinated by its head, Peter Stewart, gathered to promote this cause. Though small, this dedicated bunch made quite a contribution to Australia's support for the Ottawa Convention 1997 (which banned antipersonnel mines) signed by Alexander

Downer, then Minister for Foreign Affairs. The Australian Network to Ban Landmines was coordinated by the amazing and courageous Patricia Pak Poy, RSM, in Adelaide. I was able to meet her and a wide and rich band of people at several national conferences, learning so much about this campaign.

The Anti-Uranium Coalition of WA (AUCWA) was formed in the mid 1990s with the aim of keeping Western Australia free of uranium mining. I represented MAPW at its meetings, took the minutes and, of course, painted innumerable banners. AUCWA transitioned to ANAWA, the Anti-Nuclear Alliance of WA, when Pangea, a company promoting the need for an international repository for medium- to high-level radioactive waste in outback WA, arrived. Through our activities, the community became aware of this initiative – and was enraged. Our stalls in public places were rushed at times as people eagerly signed our petition to stop Pangea in its tracks. I think well over 50,000 signatures were gathered and Greens MLC Giz Watson's efforts for legislation to thwart the company were taken over by the two major parties, each keen to win public favour by passing prohibiting legislation. Premier Geoff Gallop regarded Labor's success on that as one of his greatest achievements. Pangea's office in Perth closed down.

When Dee Margetts was elected as a Greens senator in 1993, I took over her role as WA Coordinator for People for Nuclear Disarmament for about a year. In 2005 I again began to work with PND. Now Jo Vallentine, another former Greens senator, and I share the role of convenor. What an enormous pleasure it is to work with her and others like Mia Pepper, CCWA's nuclear-free future campaigner, and the young ones in Ban Uranium Mining Permanently (BUMP).

My favourite calico project last year was creating a large curtain portraying a wetlands scene populated by waterbirds for

Environment House in Bayswater – a sheer indulgence for one who loves feathered friends.

Climate change is a consuming interest. Urgent global action is needed and Australia is dragging its feet shamefully. Along with abolition of nuclear weapons and nuclear power, this issue truly impinges on the very survival of life on this unique and precious planet, our only home. I will try to concentrate my activism on these great challenges and continue to urge our politicians to take them more seriously by writing more letters to newspapers and no doubt whirring up more banners on my mum's ancient sewing machine.

◇◇

JUDY BLYTH *is a resident of Western Australia. She has been active in many community-based groups including Friends of the Earth, Medical Association for the Prevention of War, and People against Nuclear Disarmament. She has been creating banners since the 1980s.*

It's up to us

JAIME YALLUP FARRANT

Seven years ago you wouldn't have found me in front of a large audience calling for clear and urgent action on climate change. You wouldn't have even found me in the room. I just wasn't interested. It's not that I wasn't a good person; it's just that all of my work was about social justice and working to assist those most vulnerable in our society. But climate change? I just didn't get it.

I walked out of Al Gore's *An Inconvenient Truth*. I found it depressing and boring. When asked to get involved in climate campaigns by friends I'd get irritated by their pesky annoyances and 'Chicken Little' statements.

And now? Now I work full time as a climate campaigner. In fact, hang out with me and the conversation will soon turn to the climate, as my friends and family are finding out.

So what happened?

I could say I was born for this work. A Leo, I've always had delusions of grandeur and figured I'd accomplish something fantastic in my life, that I was destined for greatness. If you know anything about what climate science is telling us – yet still believe we can turn it around – I think you have to have a healthy dose of arrogance and be a little delusional.

At two years of age I was breaking my younger sister out of prison (OK, so it was the playpen – but she was still behind bars, right?) and climbing the cupboard to find her dummy. I was the bossy kid at school, ruling the playground and making sure people did the 'right thing'. By the age of 14 I had decided to 'do drama with naughty kids' and by 21 I was studying it at university.

I focused on exploring how kids disengaged from school and how they could use drama to re-engage. I learnt more from the kids I worked with than I ever could have hoped to teach them and my passion for social justice was embedded.

It was clear that given the right circumstances these kids could work things out for themselves. They weren't evil or damaged – they'd often had awful things to deal with and were doing the best they could. I developed a practice based on trusting the participants to find their own solutions and using the power of community.

I moved to Australia and kept working in this area. I didn't consider myself an activist or even a social justice campaigner until I attended a Students of Sustainability conference. During the conference I realised my work was a part of a much bigger story.

It was easy for me to be anti-establishment, to resist the mainstream. I grew dreadlocks, had piercings, and looked every bit as anti-establishment as I felt.

Some years later I realised this approach wasn't working for me. While I got to work in incredible places with incredible people, and do things that inspired me, ultimately there would always be another kid walking through the revolving door of the prison. I needed to address the system that kept creating these situations and, somehow, I needed to do what I could to change it.

I spent years training in creating and developing teams, leadership and management. I began to understand that if I wanted any hope of addressing the issues I could see I needed to work with others; I needed to impact the mainstream, even those I thought 'didn't care'.

I removed my dreadlocks and trained myself to work within the mainstream setting. I wore corporate clothes and consulted for big business and government. I learnt to speak their language and trained myself to understand the assumptions that made up the cultures I encountered.

However, throughout this time my focus was singularly social justice – and my perception on that was quite narrow. I 'liked' the environment, would plant trees if I got a chance, but when asked to engage in climate change initiatives or to learn more about this area, I dismissed them. Close friends were infuriated by me – how could I do so much and care so much about some issues and not about climate.

Through attending an Awakening the Dreamer Symposium – weird name I know but a friend told me I had to go – I started to question my assumptions. The symposium's purpose is to create an environmentally sustainable, socially just and spiritually fulfilling human presence on the planet. I didn't even have a spirituality (or so I thought) and, as I've said, I believed the environment was somewhere nice to visit if you got the time.

I hadn't realised it at the time, but I had the 'humans are brilliant and amazing' assumption combined with the 'technology'll fix it' assumption. With these assumptions in place I could rest easy in the knowledge that climate change really wasn't such a serious issue, and if it was a serious issue, we'd handle it with no problem. After all, we're brilliant.

Realising that those assumptions were not necessarily true,

and allowing myself to question them, led me to the path I'm now on. It also led to a fair amount of apologising and some restoration work with friends who'd been trying to get me to see sense for years.

At first it was easy to continue my work as a facilitator and trainer working in cultural change and believe I was making a difference – and in many ways I was. However, the more I read about climate change and the more I began to understand what was happening, the more I realised changing light bulbs and the 'enlightenment of the population' just wouldn't be enough.

It wasn't enough for me to be including climate change in my conversations when I got a chance. We needed as many people as possible to bring their hearts, minds and skills to this issue. Yes we still have so many other things that need our attention, but if we ignored this one, everything I cared about would be harmed.

Over the last few years or so I've reoriented everything to be within the context of climate change, and when you start doing this it's not hard – after all, everything's connected.

If in Australia we think we have an issue with refugee arrivals now, how are we going to deal with millions of displaced people throughout Asia due to rising sea levels? When we work to eradicate extreme poverty during our lifetime and do not address climate, we're ignoring what is likely to be one of the biggest contributors to extreme poverty we've ever known.

So now my life is incredibly simple, although not necessarily easy. I work to create a socially just, environmentally sustainable and spiritually fulfilling world. You can't have one without the others and, luckily, living in Nyoongar Country, I have the opportunity to learn from the oldest continuing living human culture.

In our Western world we've separated things so as to understand them. We've taken them apart like the pieces of a clock – and while that's provided some wonderful advances in medicine and technology, we've forgotten about the whole. In Nyoongar Culture there is no separation between caring for country, caring for our families, and practising our spirituality – they are one and the same.

I choose to believe we can turn things around. It's up to us. Each and every one of us.

◇◇

JAIME YALLUP FARRANT *resides with her family in Western Australia and is a climate justice campaigner working through the It's Up 2 Us Initiative and in partnership with 350.org. She works with local Aboriginal Elders to understand the connection between culture and caring for country and trains people in facilitating the Awakening the Dreamer Symposium.*

Locking the farm gates

SARAH MOLES

I've been a greenie for about 20 years. My activism was initially driven by my maternal instincts: concern for my children's future and a determination to do something to prevent us plunging over one of the cliffs at the tipping point. Now that my children are grown, I campaign for future generations.

Whether it is in creeks, lakes, rivers or wetlands, or even under the ground, water is my thing. It pushes all my buttons. As far as we know, life is impossible without it. So it's worth fighting for.

I have a deep sense of connection to and belonging in the Murray Darling Basin. From my kitchen window I can see the watershed and I take enormous pleasure from spending time on the creek that flows through my property, the rivers that bring life to the Basin's towns and the wetlands that support spectacular wildlife.

My groundwater education began in 2006 when I was appointed to the Queensland Great Artesian Basin Advisory Council (QGABAC). It was at that table that the unconventional gas industry first popped on to my radar. I'm not directly affected by unconventional gas development; the nearest wells are two or three hours' drive from my home, on some of the finest farming land in the world. The QGABAC was a representative body and

I listened carefully to what a couple of experienced and crusty water-bore drillers had to say about this burgeoning industry. To say I was alarmed by what I learnt then and over the coming months is something of an understatement.

Over the next few months I read, researched, wrote summaries of (mostly) the related environmental issues and reached out through grassroots community networks.

At that time, occasional articles about coal seam gas (CSG) were appearing in Queensland's rural press. Then well-known activist Drew Hutton began campaigning. He joined forces with conservative farmers and momentum started to build. The number of people attending rallies and protests grew. CSG and new coalmines hit the mainstream media.

At about the same time concerns were also building in New South Wales about the expansion of the coal mining industry and the new kid on the block, CSG. Over several months the Lock The Gate movement came together to actively oppose this last gasp of the fossil fuel industry. For someone frustrated by an environment movement that sometimes seemed to have forgotten what 'activism' means, it was a breath of fresh air.

The alliance between conservative farmers and left-leaning city-based environmentalists was newsworthy in its own right. The ever-growing rallies were always colourful, sometimes theatrical, usually entertaining and featured occasional stunts leading to arrests.

Love him or loathe him, radio broadcaster Alan Jones was instrumental for the Lock the Gate campaign. He MC'd community forums on Queensland's Darling Downs, and the Southern Highlands and Liverpool Plains in New South Wales. He spoke at rallies, addressed the National Press Club and used his radio program to take the issue to millions in metropolitan areas far from the gas fields. To this day he continues to interview people opposed to the industry. From across the political divide, and from economy to health to property rights to food security and beyond, people involved in diverse parts of the campaign have had access to millions of listeners.

I went to countless events and spoke at some of them. Q&A sessions and casual conversations over cups of tea revealed the diverse reasons for people's concerns. Farmers were obviously concerned about their land, water supply, and property values, and the impact on their businesses given the difficulties of co-existence. Tourism operators talked about ruined landscape values. They and people involved in manufacturing were concerned about the resources boom driving up the Aussie dollar. Doctors spoke of potential health impacts. Vets flagged impacts on livestock and even companion animals. Lawyers took issue with and raised concerns about the inequitable playing field. Across the spectrum, there was huge concern about profits going offshore. In one memorable case a farmer told me, 'I have the tiniest inkling of how the blackfellas must have felt.' And several times in several places, the patriotic card was played. 'This isn't what my father/grandfather/uncle fought for,' I heard.

And it's not.

Most of our elected parliamentarians are no longer serving the interests of those who voted them into office. They serve big business and corporate masters, and revolving doors between parliaments and industry boardrooms ensure continuity and cross-fertilisation.

We are being sold down the river and our country is being sold for a song. I can't imagine not being involved in this fight. Water is life. Without it, everything stops.

SARAH MOLES *is a mother of two living on a small property on Queensland's Darling Downs. She trained as a photographer but has spent most of the last 20 years working on environmental issues. She has passions for all things watery, particularly in the Murray Darling, Great Artesian and Lake Eyre basins.*

Kick-starters for tree planting

LOLO HOUBEIN

World War Two March 1945

We are having a meeting in the dormitory, Frans (13 years), Will (12) and 11-year-old me. We must find a way to get out of this institution in a tiny village where we and a dozen other kids are stranded because the driver of the truck took off with our identity papers. We are but one of many child transports escaping starvation in Western Holland. We are alone in the world and have lost our identities. All we have is our hunger. We decide to go on hunger strike until we get put on another truck to the promised land. All the children lie on their beds when mealtime comes. Frans, Will and I explain to the staff why we are on strike. We are told how ungrateful we are. We know. We wait. And wait. The next day we get a promise. We start eating. Will leaves first. Then Frans. Then I and the little ones. We never saw each other again. I never attempted another hunger strike.

Peacetime 1946–1947

We are building a new world, collecting donations for the Red Cross. There will never be war and hunger again. Anything is possible if you decide on a course for peace and let people know. Then the Cold War starts.

Australia 1958–1967

There are 398 voluntary organisations in South Australia catering for all of the people's needs. What's left for the government to do? I join the Good Neighbour Council and find myself organising a furniture pool for new arrivals. A political party asks me to join. That doesn't last because it's about defeating 'the others'. I have no enemies, everybody counts.

After joining Community Aid Abroad (now Oxfam) I borrow four acres of land, a farmer with machinery and I obtain free barley seed. A good crop can raise money for a new agricultural college in Gujarat, India. Activism is creeping out at night with a torch to check for barley grubs. But in that drought year the crop fails. The voluntary fire brigade burns it off for free so I can hand back clean land. Donations roll in. The Gujarati College plants an orchard. I write thank you letters because my fundraiser was a failure.

1968–1980

Raising kids, working full time, studying part time. Sending clothes to India for Tibetan refugees. I decide to always work in jobs that can make the world a better place: Community Aid Abroad, university, sheltered workshop, schools. While teaching in Darwin I join Amnesty International and join a tree planters group. I invite Al Grassby, the people-loving Minister for Immigration, to visit our high school and tell the kids what's wrong with racism. He comes the next school year and 1100 kids receive the benefit of his words. You have to trust that some fall like seeds in fertile ground. I'm back in Adelaide to see my grandson grow up, teaching English to refugees and writing books.

South Australia 1981

Partner Burr Dodd and I hear Richard St Barbe Baker on the ABC's *Science Show*. He says Earth will die unless its landmass keeps a one-third cover of trees. We look at each other. We live in a shed, are building a house. But we think this tree-planting job can be organised. We set a time limit of one year of our lives. If it takes off there'll be other people to run it. We are kick-starters, not office holders. No point in flogging unpopular causes. Should it fail we resume house building and plant trees ourselves. Night after night we read up on trees. With degrees in linguistics and classics, we know at least how to study and research. We grasp the crucial importance of trees for all life on Earth. I wish I could sit in a tree to save a forest, but I can't. But the time is ripe for this tree-planting caper. We set our own course in the science of trees, soil, seeds and propagation. We lay out a plan to re-tree South Australia by 2050, beyond our lifetime. Idealists? Realists? Friends chuckle.

A timetable eliminates worries about delays in our personal lives. We reason that the farmers have the land. Therefore city people should raise seedlings during summer that farmers can plant as the rains start. The seedlings would be free. We meet costs from membership fees. Pensioners and students willing to raise seedlings get free membership.

We draw lines on the map of South Australia, as far as there is a drop of water. If there are people in Cook there must be water to carry seedlings through the first summer, after which they are on their own.

When we hear that Richard St Barbe Baker will pass through Adelaide on his way from Kenya to New Zealand, we take the leap. Burr contacts the tree saint's hosts. The Barbe agrees to give a talk! Tree lovers organise lunches. Burr hires the North Adelaide YMCA Hall seating 400. Advertisements, flyers and Burr's car sticker, ST BARBE IS COMING, becomes a hit.

An hour before starting time all 400 seats are taken. People fill floor space and pack the sides of the podium. St Barbe walks in leaning on a cane; he's nearly 90. On seeing the crowds he straightens up, strides to the podium and delivers his passionate plea for Earth to be repaired with trees, to not let it die. A standing throng listens in the hallway. Outside people press ears to windows.

Afterwards we and friends stand ready with pens and notepads, taking details of 200 people wanting to become members of South Australia's Men of the Trees. We set a date for the first meeting a fortnight later in the same hall, already reserved. During that meeting groups form, covering many suburbs. People with amazingly appropriate skills and knowledge take on positions in groups, on the committee and in the field. In naming one, I honour them all: Betty Westwood, the 'Tree Lady', inspired us all.

We work along with them for a year-and-a-half. One special meeting changes the name to Trees for Life. With farming and tree planting still a male domain, Burr is the public profile while in our shed home I answer the telephone that never stops and do letter campaigns to regions slow to take up offers of free trees. Periodically we drive our utility campervan to farms whose owners expressed interest. Their main question is: 'What will it cost?' When we say the trees are free, some ask, 'What's in it for you?' Farmers didn't see many idealists then. We explain the profit trees bring to land, livestock, crops and Earth itself and how easy they are to raise. Explaining it in economic terms we take our cue from E.F. Schumacher's *Small Is Beautiful*.

Within a few years, membership hits 10,000. Tree planting becomes so popular that politicians roll up, sign up, plant trees. Schoolchildren are raising trees. Thousands of city dwellers raise as many boxes of 60 trees as they like. Many become friends with their farmers and grow trees until the farm is revegetated, birds return, ecosystems function again. Trees for Life car stickers are everywhere.

We return to house building and raise boxes of trees for some 20 years. Trees for Life has changed the landscape of South Australia. Travelling throughout the state I have seen the different ages of tree plantings and know the Earth is being repaired. But due to logging, Australia has only 19 per cent forest cover, second lowest after the Middle East. Trees for Life celebrated its 30th anniversary in 2011, as strong as ever with a dedicated staff and volunteers and its own Westwood nursery. Farmers have planted over 30 million trees.

After such an experience it is hard not to think that it is possible to make the world a better place. I've used the 'recipe' of taking a year of my life to kick-start an idea until it flies or sinks. It worked again with a branch of Sydney's Wrap With Love, an Australian network of women knitting hundreds of thousands of wraps for people who suffer cold. Wrap With Love SA spread to around 50 suburbs and to country towns. Again, there were skilled people running groups, providing storage, holding exhibitions, packing boxes, and driving to carriers who deliver the wraps for free to the Sydney warehouse where aid organisations collect them.

Time to do the rest of my activism by writing. With half a dozen books published, I gathered my know-how of growing food at home and wrote the book for my grandchildren because the writing was on the wall that the future of food was in jeopardy.

One Magic Square: Grow Your Own Food on One Square Metre appeared in August 2008 and for seven years I preached the gospel of organic food growing on the speakers' circuit. The companion volume, *Outside The Magic Square: A Handbook for Food Security*, was launched in 2012 by activist chef Simon

Bryant, new director of Tasting Australia, who stops both waste and want. The books do their work as people become food-wise in home gardens, community gardens and, hopefully, on farms. No one should have to face a wild weather future without food security at home.

In my 80th year I was fortunate to give workshops on gardening at school and at home to country schoolteachers and students. These workshops were supported by Natural Resources Management in the Murray–Darling Basin SA, OPAL, the Diggers' Club and Neutrog Fertilisers.

Just when we thought it time to sit on our few laurels, disturbing events with farmland and mining in eastern states reached South Australian borders. It appears that no matter how long individuals work to repair the Earth that feeds us, our governments can slap mining exploration and excavation licences on anyone's land. Mining can undo generations of conservation and tree planting work within a year, as well as spoil water supplies. To help protect farming and conservation land, Burr and I joined the Lock The Gate movement to facilitate the distribution of Lock The Gate signs for landholders. Coal, iron, gold and other profitable substances cannot sustain us into the future like farms can. Hence the new South Australian Land Protection Association (SALPA), the new activism of desperation!

◇◇

LOLO HOUBEIN AM *is an award-winning author whose works include* One Magic Square: Grow your Own Food on One Square Metre *and* Outside the Magic Square: A Handbook for Food Security. *She and partner Burr Dodd kick-started the movement that became Trees for Life SA in 1981. She is working on a book that looks at food security during climate change.*

Long-service leave for activists

BRENDA CONOCHIE

As the eldest daughter of activist parents, I was destined/doomed to a life dominated by activism. From the time they met in the late 1940s, my folks' fervent hopes for a world without war, racism or inequality seemed to be catered for by communism, for which they worked very hard. But reports of how many people Stalin had killed or starved pretty much smashed that 'ism' for them, and the Soviet tanks rolling through Budapest in 1956 rolled through their hearts. So they turned their attention to making the world a better place in other ways.

Mum threw herself into feminism in the heady days of the mid 70s, particularly the push to rid the education system of sexist books, sex bias in subjects offered, teachers' 'dress' requirements (as in 'Wear a dress, not those trousers, please. Sure it's 17 degrees at school today but don't stockings keep women's legs warm?'). When they found themselves in a suburban empty nest, they worked with my aunt and uncle to start the Wolery Ecological Community on the south coast of WA. It's still going strong today with its 15 households. As Dad put it, he wanted to live the rest of his life as if The Revolution he'd hoped and strived for had actually happened.

As for me, as well as Abschol tutoring at university, working hard to end Australian involvement in and conscription for the Vietnam War, co-founding a little playcentre for disadvantaged kids in East Perth in 1974, and marching for social justice issues over the years, my activism until the year 2000 was primarily in the nuclear disarmament and environmental movements, particularly the movement against uranium mining. I combined this activism with mostly part-time teaching work, a little song writing and performing around the traps, and parenting my two daughters – who made more than one complaint about taking phone calls while the rice burned.

In late 2000, I co-founded, with my partner Rob Gulley and friend Rachael Roberts, Environment House, in an inner Perth suburb. The idea was to create a public-access place that would bring together three services:

- 'how-to' information and training on what we call 'SustainAbilities' (slashing energy and water use, turning foodscraps to fertiliser, detoxifying the home);
- the sale of small eco-products, alternatives to 'eco-hostile' supermarket products;
- information and petitions on local and global environmental campaigns (uranium mining, forest protection, GM, and climate change).

Our hope was that people might come in for one or other of these services, but broaden their focus to the other two.

We gathered a good-sized body of supporters, some of whom paid the rent between them for about seven years. Rachael was the bold, can-do, strategic thinker, inspiring financial commitments from people in her circles.

We established and kept up a cracking pace, with 90 per cent volunteer labour – plus the odd grant when we got lucky – enabling us to pay one or two people a part-time pittance at times (we reckon if you pay peanuts, you get passion!). Environment House was a real shop in a main street, and we kept it open all day Monday to Saturday. Thousands of people who knew nothing about us would drop in, attracted by the murals or the range of products in the window, asking, 'So what's all this about, eh?' That was music to our ears. It's why we were there; it made the long hard work worthwhile.

From 2004 we managed to win a series of grants and contracts from state, federal and local governments on the theme of energy efficiency. We developed a professional energy auditing arm, culminating in a big contract with the Western Australian utility Synergy. It was funded by the state government to provide home energy and water audits with installation of eco-hardware (plus, for most, new fridges for old) for 4000 homes in financial hardship. Rob and I, and our team of bookings people and 14 energy auditors, gave this our all for 15 months until the scheme was axed, mid-contract, when the WA government decided to divert this money for an election promise of one dollar a week off the bills of healthcare cardholders and seniors, regardless of income. This was a king hit.

So many people around town interpreted news of this axing to mean that we'd been 'closed down by the government'. We had to explain patiently, 'No, we are still here, going back to doing what we did for the first few years, with no grants, running our compost workshops, shop and stalls at markets, fairs, fetes and festivals, offering free information and useful eco-products at the best prices in town.'

After our shop rent was suddenly doubled from its original $1000 a month we moved, in 2009, to a little house and shed next to a lake and the Swan River, with low rent ($250 per month), courtesy of the City of Bayswater, WA. The downside of our otherwise pleasant little shop-in-a-house, with its native garden in the front and backyard food garden, is that it's not zoned commercial so Council will only allow us to advertise Saturday opening hours, and we don't have much passing trade. However, we still do stalls at markets, fairs, fetes and festivals most weekends, to be 'out in people's faces', bringing our three offerings – products, petitions and sustainability support.

We now feel we are at a kind of crossroad. Our shop only just breaks even. Should we keep doing the same things? More of the eco products we sell are appearing in supermarkets and hardware stores. If it was only about the products, I feel it would not be worth continuing. But it's the link and the leverage from the products to living with a much smaller footprint that is so badly needed, and the petitions we keep on the counter and circulate to our customers (e.g., buyers of palm-oil-free soap products) who've agreed to be on our e-list. 'Products as portal to eco-activism' perhaps.

Looking back, it's clear that in our situation, beholden as we've been to state, federal and local government grants most of the time, our ability to speak out has been badly short-changed as we fretted about how our current or future grants or contracts would be affected. But I, at least, feel that much more speaking out is needed on many fronts in Australia in the years ahead.

How to entice people through this portal? Make it all sound like fun or a challenge? Be a bit cheeky? Hide the despair we feel about climate change, the government's green light for the opening of WA's first uranium mines after 30 years of successful campaigning to 'Keep it in the ground', the ramping up of native forest destruction, the impending construction of polluting mega-incinerators for our household waste, the increasing hold of corporations like Monsanto over our agriculture in WA, the slash and burn of so many eco-initiatives in the Abbott–Hockey budget of May 2014?

Or admit to the D(espair) word and concentrate on strategies for dealing with it?

We need to provide a safe space with healthy boundaries within which effective action can happen. A lot of our visitors/ customers are youngish parents who need to be energetic and optimistic with their kids. They can't afford to have their energy, time and love of life sapped by the despair of full-frontal examination of what's going on. But they are keen to do something.

In the 1980s, psychologists recommended that those fearful about the Cold War turning hot and nuclear should *do* something – march, make badges or posters – as an antidote to despair. It was considered helpful for children to see their parents doing something. Kids aged nine to 12, before they are totally distracted by their hormones, can be passionate about the state of the planet or the fate of endangered species and need outlets for these concerns. They could attend multi-age, banner-making workshops. Then kids would contribute to artwork, and people's passion, clearly set out on calico, might be seen on TV and help melt the hearts of environmental decision-makers. Or groups could meet to research and prepare letters and submissions on ecological issues.

What's in it for this BOA (Burnt Out Activist)? If more people contributed a little, some hyper-activists could step back, maybe take long-service leave in a camper van to visit kids and grandchildren and elderly parents.

It is important to inform adults and their children that a little activism can be incorporated into family life; that a truly balanced life means living well while helping preserve life on the planet for future generations.

BRENDA CONOCHIE, *daughter of Enid and Ian Conochie, has kept alight their activism, as has her sister Kerin Booth in Tasmania. In 2000 she co-founded Environment House (Perth) with partner Rob Gulley and friend Rachael Roberts. In 2015, she's living with her widower dad (90) near Denmark WA, doing admin work for Environment House on Saving Water, Waste & Power projects (mostly involving Rob) and volunteering at Denmark Environment Centre.*

Saving Lake Claremont – a full-time job

HEIDI HARDISTY

When I first moved to Australia I joined the local Friends of Lake Claremont group. When I set off on this journey, I had no idea where it would take me. Had I realised what I was getting into, I may have decided against it. But having done it, I believe it is the best thing I have done.

I grew up in the Canadian Prairies, with its extreme weather conditions. Temperatures range from +40°C to –40°C. On many a cold winter night as a little girl, I would stare at a koala poster on my basement wall and dream of visiting the land down under. It wasn't until 2006, after a short career as a petroleum engineer, completing a MSc in aquatic population ecology, starting a family and following my husband around the world, that we arrived with our two boys in Perth, Western Australia.

Here began another amazing journey. Although I knew nothing of my strange new surroundings in the western suburbs of Perth, I soon developed a great appreciation of the unique plant and animal life. Just down the road was Lake Claremont, a Conservation Category Wetland and Bush Forever Site. In fact, I soon learned that the entire south-west corner of the state was one of 34 global biodiversity hotspots. It sounded impressive, but I had no idea what it meant. When I discovered it was a hotspot because over 70 per cent of this wondrous land had already been cleared, it sparked a great interest and determination to learn more and contribute to its protection and enhancement.

It didn't take long for my neighbours to discover my passion for conservation and volunteering, and they invited me to join the Friends of Lake Claremont, which was founded in 2003 by Soozie Ross, a local resident. Before I knew it, I was running the group. I needed to learn more so I started to take courses (like Introduction to Bush Regeneration and City Bush Guides) and attend related seminars.

I could not imagine how much we would come to achieve in six short years. I simply took it step-by-step, and took the opportunities as they presented themselves. Since 2009 we have been awarded 17 grants totalling $467,700 and, if all goes according to plan, by the end of 2016 we will be responsible for planting over 270,000 native seedlings, helping to restore wetland and bushland.

At this point you may be wondering how I find the time. Well I am fortunate in that my husband supports me so I choose to contribute to society as a full-time volunteer. This has drawbacks, as I find working from home can sometimes mean longer hours than if I were paid. Since there is no support staff, running a 'Friends of' group sometimes means doing too many jobs. The first few years of leading the group were very stressful at times due to my inexperience. But I am determined and have a strong work ethic. The group is growing, currently it has over 100 financial members, and is slowly building a core working team of active volunteers including a fundraising coordinator, grants officer, webmaster, newsletter editor, hand-weeding group and a tea team.

When I joined the group in 2006, the FOLC were active

hosting monthly busy bees and special events like Clean Up Australia Day and National Tree Day. I wanted to help raise awareness about Lake Claremont and wetlands in general, and help people, especially children, to reconnect with nature and contribute to their community. I began to ask questions of our group and to meet regularly with the Supervisor of Parks and Gardens for the Town of Claremont. I discovered that with no fewer than six schools in the area there was great potential for school participation.

After many discussions and investigations, I started the Year 10 Community Service Program in 2009 with two local private schools, Scotch College and Christ Church Grammar School. The boys are required to do volunteer work as part of their high school program. Now most Friday afternoons we have a group of 15 to 20 boys helping with various projects around the lake consistent with our mission of protecting and enhancing the area.

In that same year, 2009, several other important events happened that would lead to great change. First, the Town of Claremont held a public referendum that resulted in the decision to close the golf course and create a 21-hectare park. This meant the backing of the community for a new park and the opportunity to restore over 10 hectares of native vegetation. At the same time, I met Claire Brittain who was serving with me on the Lake Claremont Committee. She also had many years experience in volunteering, especially in administration. With the help of our high school students, we had the manpower to tackle more projects. Now all we needed was money. We determined that there were community grants around but we needed to be incorporated to win them. With Claire's expertise, the FOLC became a Company Limited by Guarantee. That enabled us to apply for and win our first Community Action Grant, $20,000 from the federal government's Caring for Our Country program to restore a 2500-square-metre portion of the wetland buffer. In 2010, over 10,000 seedlings were planted with the help of over 200 volunteers. Despite one of the hottest summers on record, over 70 per cent of the plants survived.

The following year we won the same Caring for Our Country grant to continue restoring the wetland buffer and began to build our volunteer network. In 2011, I was in charge of 700 volunteers, including 500 primary school children, to plant 14,000 seedlings. We hosted two massive planting days, one with a group called the Big Help Mob who planted 3700 seedlings in three hours, and National Tree Day with members of the public who came from near and far, planting 2000.

At the same time the Town of Claremont began developing a weed management program with our help, so the seedlings were thriving. And thanks to Claire's new expertise in applying for grants, huge success followed over the next several years. We won three more Caring for Our Country grants to restore the wetland buffer, increasing the total to $139,000. We also won two Community Action grants from the WA Department of Environment and Conservation totalling $66,000 to restore portions of both the wetland bed and buffer. In 2014 we acquired a Swan River Trust ALCOA Landcare Program worth $17,600, bringing us closer to completing the planting in the wetland buffer, estimated to be 2017.

But that's not all! We also turned our attention to revegetating more than five hectares of the closed golf course. From 2011–2015 we won five consecutive grants from the State Natural Resource Management Program to reconstruct native woodland – totalling $217,800.

Involving over 1000 volunteers and more than 50 planting

sessions each year, the numbers of seedlings planted have been impressive: in 2012 we planted 46,800 seedlings; 2013 – 83,000; 2014 – 59,300; and 2015 – 32,275.

Each year I continue to coordinate, lead and build on this network of volunteers from the local and wider communities including the Big Help Mob, corporations, church groups and students from local schools and universities. Initially some of the grants had a small proportion for labour costs, so I have partnered with Conservation Volunteers Australia. CVA has helped establish relationships with corporations plus a group called the Shah Satnam Ji Green 'S' Welfare Force Wing. The latter planted over 37,000 seedlings for us in the three years 2013–2015.

We now have a good system for handling massive groups of volunteers by dividing them into groups of 10 to 15 with a FOLC team leader and designated planting area. We always provide a small educational component, telling our 'guests' about the history of the area, the projects we are undertaking and about the importance of our remnant wetlands and bushlands. We get a great response and support from the local schools, residents and organisations who come back every year to participate.

It is worth noting the projects would not have happened without the long-term relationship and support that the FOLC have had from the local council and staff of the Town of Claremont. It is also significant that the Town of Claremont already had a management plan in place for Lake Claremont, thanks to local councillor and resident Bruce Haynes. The cooperation and support between the Town and the Friends must be worked on and not taken for granted, as councillors move on and there are always budget considerations. Part of the reason we are winning state and federal grants is because the Town of Claremont generally matches funds by way of infrastructure (like fencing and footpaths), mulch and herbicide spraying for the control of weeds. Overall, it has been a tremendous relationship.

Our ultimate goal is to have a healthy wetland and bushland that will largely maintain itself. In 2010, the pink fairy orchid appeared in the remnant bushland for the first time in years. A positive sign of things to come.

◇◇

HEIDI HARDISTY *has won a number of Western Australian and national awards for her volunteer work in leading and inspiring hundreds of volunteers in the continual restoration of Lake Claremont. In 2013 she received the National Pride of Australia Medal – Environment Category.*

A river, a bridge and a struggle

RICHARD OWEN

I am not a born leader, just a person who wants to improve things in whatever field I have worked.

Way back in the 1960s, I trained as a secondary teacher; a geography teacher as it happened. From my educational beginnings I was concerned about independent learning and the processes of skill acquisition needed to become what is currently termed a 'lifelong learner'. Along the way I have always encouraged students to enquire for themselves.

I took some time out to study theology and then returned to teaching at the time secondary library resource centres were being funded across Australia. I became a teacher-librarian in a new open-plan high school in the dormitory suburbs north of Adelaide. This provided an opportunity to further develop the independent learning skills of students and teachers. The programs we developed, which came to be called 'information literacy', were considered national leaders in their field.

In 1980 our family purchased a beach shack at the mouth of the River Murray in an area known as the Coorong. In 1981, the mouth of the river closed for the first time in recorded history. Since then it has never been far from closing. Water extraction upstream had exceeded the river's ability to survive. We started planting native plants clandestinely around the area, making a few mistakes in the process, but learning all the time.

While still working for the state government – I was by then working in TAFE as deputy head of the Centre for Applied Learning Systems – I became involved with people in the Murray Mouth area who had, since 1993, been resisting a proposal to build a bridge from Goolwa to Hindmarsh Island to replace a cable ferry service. Developers of the Hindmarsh Island marina needed a bridge to be built if their proposal was to proceed beyond Stage 1. We formed a local organisation called Friends of Goolwa and Kumarangk (*Kumarangk* was the local Aboriginal name for Hindmarsh Island). I was the chairperson of this group from its inception, and took our concerns about the bridge/region to the Conservation Council of South Australia (CCSA), the umbrella organisation for environmental non-government organisations in South Australia. The CCSA was willing to support us. I was invited to come onto the CCSA Board and remained there for the next 10 years, right through the litigation related to the bridge.

I had retired late in 1998, aged 52, and by this time was enmeshed in the Hindmarsh Island bridge affair. I had really enjoyed the challenges provided by education, but was realising there was much else to become involved in.

Both the CCSA and The Friends of Kumarangk were sued by the developers of the Hindmarsh Island marina. A Strategic Litigation Against Public Participation (SLAPP) suit was used against the community. This is intended to censor, intimidate and silence critics by burdening them with the cost of a legal defence until they abandon their opposition. Letters were sent out by the developers threatening legal action against all kinds of people in the local community. We were about to be introduced to the legal system with all of its foibles. The CCSA was sued on

18 grounds and won on 17 of these. The 18th went to the full bench of the Supreme Court in South Australia and lost in a split decision, 2:1. The CCSA then tried to take the final ground to the High Court but the High Court refused to hear us. Nonetheless, despite winning almost all of the case, the CCSA still had to pay the developers $50,000.

The local Aboriginal people, the Ngarrindjeri, had not been consulted by the developers, and were also opposing the bridge. We stood together in opposition, along with the Construction, Forestry, Mining and Energy Union, the CFMEU.

Acting on evidence of significant Aboriginal sites, Robert Tickner, then Labor Minister for Aboriginal Affairs, placed a 25-year ban on bridge construction in July 1994. John Howard took power in 1996 and soon had the *Hindmarsh Island Bridge Act* passed, which exempted the bridge location from the protection provided by the federal *Aboriginal and Torres Strait Islanders Heritage Protection Act 1984*. The bridge went ahead. It was opened in 2001. Later, the Ngarrindjeri people defeated the developers in the Federal Court, overturning a state Royal Commission that claimed the Ngarrindjeri were liars and had been manipulated by environmentalists. But, by then of course, the bridge had been built.

It was during this time that I wrote an academic paper about the way we had used 'information literacy' in the bridge struggle. It was published in the Australian Library Journal, the professional journal of the Australian Library and Information Association (ALIA). Shortly after, ALIA was threatened with legal action by the developers. Some months later I was approached by an international publisher seeking permission to reprint this article in an international publication on 'information literacy'. I refused them permission at that time, probably because I felt intimidated by the huge litigation effort (the largest in Australian history) being pursued by the developers of the marina here, and didn't want to cause more problems for unsuspecting people.

Just prior to retiring, we had purchased a small sand dune and wetland property (now Tarni Warra sanctuary) on the Murray River's edge, which we intended to restore, covenant and declare a private sanctuary. During the bridge fight we had been challenged by one of the local farmers for being city-based 'greenies' who did nothing constructive for the environment. We intended to rehabilitate our 15 acres, but after doing that realised there was an island needing restoration too, so along with the Hindmarsh Island Landcare Group we created the Murray Mouth Estuary Restoration (MMER) Project in 2001. This project by 2013 has propagated and planted over 340,000 plants of more than 80 local species on more than 80 sites across the island and Sir Richard Peninsula. I have been the project co-ordinator since the MMER Project began. Reconnecting natural environments that are increasingly disconnected will be an essential part of the habitat restoration needed if we are to cope with climate change.

For the past three years our local Landcare group has also been an active part of the Community Nurseries Network, a network of up to eight community nurseries spread around the Lower Lakes, the Murray Mouth and the Coorong. Most were established using federal funding and aim to address the consequences of the millennium drought. Community-driven and managed, but funded through the state Environment Department via the Goolwa to Wellington Local Action Planning Association, this has been a highly successful collaboration.

All of this has been about social activism for me: empowering people, protecting and rehabilitating the environment, recognising the opportunities for constructive change and running with them.

What have we learned? First, don't panic and make sure you are well organised. When we stopped jet-skis in the Coorong National Park, we took on the boating industry in this state. We won, but we had to push tardy bureaucrats in the state Environment Department to act once the decision had been made: park rangers to put up the appropriate signage in the park to inform the public of these changes; and the local police to act when this was being contravened.

Second, make sure your intelligence is accurate, not hearsay. To act on second, third or fourth hand information often causes distress and angst for supporters. Don't believe the rumours; try to confirm the facts.

Third, provide information so your people are well aware of the reason they are acting and are better informed than their opponents. This applies in whatever context you are working. People are empowered by having access to relevant information and should be more prepared to act.

Fourth, take steps to inform and warn about legal issues early. If your campaign is likely to have legal implications, seek sound legal advice so that participants can be aware of what could happen. There are sympathetic lawyers and experienced activists around who will often provide this early support *pro bono*.

Fifth, if there is likely to be confrontation, train in non-violent direct action techniques. Again, there are activists in our communities who can assist with this type of training.

Finally, collaborate. You will find there are many people with similar interests and concerns out there. You are rarely alone. One of the major strengths of the Hindmarsh Island bridge campaign was the coalition of community groups and organisations prepared to support each other.

The need for environmental activism will never cease for there is always so much to be done. There is the risk that what has been achieved may be diminished or overturned by ignorant and greedy people who are generally unaware of what we have done to Australia these past 225 years. Climate change, coupled with unbridled population growth, means that the consequences of not acting are becoming increasingly dangerous as each year passes.

◇◇

RICHARD OWEN *trained as a teacher and developed a commitment to lifelong learning. He later worked at TAFE as Deputy Head of the Centre for Applied Learning Systems. He is a co-founder of the Friends of Goolwa and Kumarangk and the Murray Mouth Estuary Restoration (MMER), a project of the Hindmarsh Island Landcare Group Inc.*

There is room for everyone in the puzzle

MIA PEPPER

A wise man who had survived the invasion of Tibet once told me, 'Don't feel sorry for me. Don't take on my troubles. You can do nothing to help. If you are compelled by my story, go home and find out what is happening there.' I was 15 and, on this rare occasion, I did what I was told.

After some investigation of our history of colonisation I began to see what was simmering beneath the surface of mainstream Australia. I was drawn to the immense injustice inflicted on Aboriginal nations across the country: the massacres, germ warfare, slavery, taking of children, dislocation from country, and theft of land and resources. It wasn't until hearing the real-life accounts, saw massacre sites and felt the unrest alive in the landscape that I began to understand the extent of the damage inflicted. I am forever learning old stories and, sadly, new ones.

I learnt about the laws that made it legal to continue to disconnect people from their country and destroy sacred places, like the *Native Title Act*, which allows mining rights to override native title rights. I learnt that our government lists old gold mines on the national heritage register and yet almost every state and territory has laws that give consent to legally and wilfully destroy Aboriginal sites of cultural and spiritual significance.

From these lessons, mining soon dominated my thoughts: the power mining companies wield, the influence they have over governments and the mass destruction they inflict on the country, the huge volumes of resources they consume and the insidious impact they have on communities worldwide. It was too much to think about without taking action.

Action has taken many different forms. I have acted with many individuals, in groups and non-government organisations. I have been involved in collective direct action, from walking on to mine sites and power plants, occupying offices and locking-on to machinery, to in-depth community work. From corporate campaigning, protest at conferences and shareholder activism at annual general meetings, to sitting at the table with mining companies and government. It is impossible to say what works and what doesn't; all these different actions are like pieces of a puzzle.

Direct actions are often amazing and inspiring acts of defiance against a system that is broken; where bringing people together with a common aim can make powerful and unexpected things happen, things you cannot plan for or quantify.

One morning after a wild dust and rain storm at Lake Cowal, in central western NSW, over a hundred people were led into the open-cut goldmine by two young Wiradjuri boys – fearless against security guards who cautioned us for trespassing. One of the boys, aged about 11, replied, 'You're the one who is trespassing. This is Wiradjuri land.' People locked-on to the dump truck named 'Jaws'. Others were dancing on mined-out rubble to the Kev Carmody song 'Thou shalt not steal', a dance piece choreographed by a dancer from the Aboriginal Tent Embassy. We stayed for hours asking for one last dance but eventually were bussed out under police escort with only a few arrests. We closed that mine for the day, possibly even the whole weekend, at huge cost and embarrassment to the company. We hadn't planned this action but had just brought those people together and so it evolved.

I have had many teachers and mentors who have shown me the importance of community work, respecting Aboriginal people of different areas and their sovereignty. I have come to see my role in community work as an environmental educator, an informant to communities and someone to help people comment on, speak out about and give feedback to government processes.

In Wiluna, a remote town on the edge of the Western Desert in WA, Toro Energy are planning to develop a network of uranium mines across two lake systems. All the announcements about the project are published in the *West Australian*. Wiluna, 600 kilometres north of Kalgoorlie, does not get the newspaper. When Toro came for public consultation on the Environmental Management Plans in Wiluna, they held the meeting on an Aboriginal funeral day. The process is fundamentally skewed in favour of mining companies, who benefit from division and poor consultation; a process allowed by a lack of government regulation. We at the Conservation Council of WA (CCWA) have a role in providing information to the entire community, whether pro or anti-mining, about the process and about management plans, the risks and impacts. It is important to avoid divisive politics of mining and communities, and to respect the autonomy and sovereignty of Aboriginal communities.

We are at a unique point in history where corporate campaigning on mining can be the most effective tool in the box. Especially when you look at the prices of coal and uranium, both of which are dropping dramatically.

Recently the CCWA commissioned an economic analysis of Toro Energy and their Wiluna project. The report exposed the economic risk of the project showing the value of the mineral as well as the risk and uncertainty of community opposition, further costs, delays and significant environmental aspects. The report confirmed the project is a bad investment. We've distributed it everywhere, to investors, banks, shareholders and government. We've consistently used economic arguments, quoting industry back to industry, and it now seems the language we've used is seeping into the media. Toro, despite having some environmental approvals, cannot progress because of funding.

Engaging in the environmental assessment process has also added pressure. The Wiluna project is subject to 35 conditions that will add to the operating costs and to the level of uncertainty for investors. It is a hard time for new miners to attract investors. So there is a great opportunity to exploit weakness, add roadblocks and exacerbate risk.

There are opportunities within politics and any opportunity for change is worth pursuing. In the case of the Toro Wiluna uranium proposal, working with government and staying engaged in the process has been useful, but will not be the deciding factor in whether the project goes ahead or not. As a result of some strong submissions, consistent challenging of approvals and lobbying of government, the conditions were strengthened at a huge cost to the company. Many people in government, industry and the media are convinced this mine will not proceed.

Action breaks the deafening silence over extreme injustice and destruction. Sometimes we break through, sometimes we wait it out and win. There is room for everyone in the puzzle.

MIA PEPPER *is the Nuclear Free Campaigner at the Conservation Council of WA and Deputy Chair of the Mineral Policy Institute.*

Voices from the Kimberley

JAN LEWIS, FIONA DEAN, DARYL DEAN,
ALI BATTEN, LAHEA LEVI

Jan Lewis

Broome is a coastal town of less than 20,000 people in the Kimberley region of Western Australia. Forty-five kilometres north of the town, up a red dirt road, is a breathtakingly beautiful spot called James Price Point. It's where the Western Australian government decided that 'Australian icon' Woodside should build the second largest liquid natural gas processing plant in the world.

This is the story of how a disparate group of community members – mothers, tradespeople, students, artists, retirees and others – combined to use their energy, skills, experience and networks to defend their families, environment and lifestyle from ruthless politicians who had never asked if the project was wanted. A few campaigners were old hands – for the many who had never marched in the street, asked a question at a shire meeting, written a letter to a politician, or defied an instruction given by a police officer, it was a life-changing experience.

Broome is different from other towns. It's formed from a delicious blend of Aboriginal, South East Asian and European cultures, hippies, artists and other escapees from mainstream city life. The laid-back lifestyle is promoted by the tourism industry. The prospect of a major development on our doorstep really brought into focus the key question for all residents: what kind of town do we want Broome to be?

In reality, despite the Western Australian government's claims to the contrary, there were a wide range of environmental and cultural reasons why the Woodside project should not proceed. The opposition of the site's traditional owners (TOs) was strong and convincing. After all, their grandfather, Mr Paddy Roe, had received an Order of Australia medal for the preservation of his country's cultural values! Most residents had visited the Pilbara and seen the impacts that major resource development projects bring. They were concerned that basing 8000 construction workers so near to town would lead to increased drug use, sexually transmitted diseases and prostitution; that housing/rental market prices would skyrocket; the plant would discharge toxic air pollution on our children; Indigenous tourism businesses on the Dampier Peninsula would suffer; and access to favourite camping and fishing spots would be lost.

Residents were also dubious about the supposed benefits of the project. People did not believe that the revenue generated would be spent in the Kimberley or that local people would get the jobs. They heard evidence from Karratha that suggested small businesses would probably fail to compete with larger external operators.

By early 2010, various local and national groups opposed to the project were active. Environmental groups and Save the Kimberly began running strong awareness-raising campaigns emphasising the environmental values of the coastal habitat. The Hands Off Country blog provided local information; small groups such as the Hub Caps were beginning direct action. Recognition of the need to create a forum for residents concerned about the social impacts of the project and to ensure all local protest activities were coordinated led to the formation of Broome Community NO GAS Campaign (BCNGC). It was not incorporated (to avoid the possibility of being sued) and had no fixed leadership apart from a treasurer. Information was shared, ideas for possible actions and events discussed, decisions taken and volunteers identified who would make things happen at the weekly NO GAS meeting.

The Campaign had three stated aims:

- to raise awareness about the impacts of the project;
- to delay the investigation works that Woodside was planning; and
- to stop the project.

Campaigners agreed to adopt the philosophy of non-violent direct action and several training workshops were held to ensure people were familiar with the tactics and strategies this encompassed. Legal training workshops were also held so people were clear what their rights were in relation to police actions.

The early phase of the campaign focused on building opposition via community education. Pamphlets, maps and photos were prepared and distributed via information stalls in shopping centres, markets and street stalls. Information nights and community rallies were held. Twelve thousand signatures were collected on postcards, which were dispatched to the Prime Minister by camel (no reply was ever received). Fences, roofs and waste bins were adorned with a creative range of NO GAS messages. The issue was continually raised on radio programs – a particular highlight being when a talkback caller on ABC radio asked Premier Barnett to resign because he was imposing the project on the Broome community despite their obvious opposition.

As resistance strengthened, BCNG Campaign established a website and Facebook site (by the time of Woodside's withdrawal the FB site had more than 4000 supporters) and paid to insert a fortnightly column in the local newspaper to counter Woodside's propaganda. A group of more than 50 people wrote lobbying letters to stakeholders every month for over a year. Many more wrote submissions in response to government project plans and the proponent's planning applications. Numerous questions were asked at Shire meetings in an attempt to ensure the Shire's policy of opposition to the project until all concerns were addressed was maintained. Politicians and visiting dignitaries, such as the WA premier and the governor-general, were lobbied to ensure they were aware of community views.

The campaign also made strong efforts to ensure Broome residents were clear about the value of the country that would be destroyed. In collaboration with Goolarabooloo traditional owners, events were organised at the proposed site at James Price Point: walks through the dune country to learn about monsoon vine thickets, storytelling about the Dreamtime stories and the song cycle that passed through the country, tree planting, etc. People were encouraged to camp with traditional owners so that Woodside activity could be monitored. A number of community science projects were also established which produced evidence to counter the claims by the WA government and their consultants that whales did not swim near the coast and bilbies were not found in the area.

The second aspect of the campaign aimed to stop the on-site testing work. Every hour that investigative drilling or surveys could be delayed was regarded as a win. Direct action took the form of blockading the convoy of Woodside employers and contractors that early each day headed out to undertake survey work. A blockade camp was established at Manari Road corner, about 20 kilometres out of town. Residents were encouraged either to camp there overnight or be there early each morning to stand in front of security officers employed to 'protect' the convoy, and demand to see the permits allowing workers to clear the site or damage registered Aboriginal heritage sites (which they did not have). In June 2011, the convoy was turned back for 30 consecutive days until more than 80 black-shirted riot squad police officers were flown in from Perth to bully and barge a path through protestors, thus allowing the bulldozing equipment to reach the site. Twenty-six people, including Aboriginal women, long-standing Broome community members and business owners were arrested and charged with criminal offences on that day.

Although some people found the police behaviour deeply distressing, the resolve to resist was not diminished and a number of tree sits, pole sits and lock-ons occurred over the following months to halt equipment and/or prevent bulldozers reaching the project site. One very successful action that generated nationwide publicity for the media-named 'lock-on grannies', occurred in May 2012 when two older Broome residents, both grandmothers, locked themselves to an old car, delaying the passage of the convoy for the day.

Due to the continued police presence on the roads leading to the project site and a conviction that BCNGC had been infiltrated, surveillance and planning for direct actions that blocked the road were, of necessity, highly secretive. Yet there was also a need to mobilise people to support the frontline. This was solved by an alert system disseminated by mobile phone to the more than 250 people willing to actively respond. Blue, yellow and red alerts were issued, with RED meaning move immediately to the location specified. A subgroup of campaigners worked to issue media releases, ensuring the campaign messages were clear and factual, and that the media had access to a local spokesperson (to counter the government claim that protestors were feral blow-ins). Another subgroup provided support for those arrested.

Without doubt it would have been more difficult to win this campaign had local residents and traditional owners not worked in collaboration with others. Visits by musicians such as John Butler, businessmen like Geoffrey Cousins, and organisations such as Sea Shepherd raised the profile of the struggle, particularly with eastern states media, and helped to raise Campaign funds. The involvement of university-based scientists enhanced the credibility of the environmental values of the site and the global importance of the dinosaur footprints. Campaigners from other parts of Australia, willing to suspend their lives and camp in the bush for months at a time, provided useful surveillance information and built the pool of people available for arrestable direct actions. The successful legal challenge by The Wilderness Society against the environmental go-ahead for the project, given by the WA Environmental Protection Authority, was a huge boost to community morale and vindicated all the time spent writing submissions. The advocacy work with Woodside's joint venture partners by environmental groups was immensely useful, as was funding that allowed BCNG members to travel to Canberra to lobby decision-makers. Our thanks go out to these people who helped a local campaign get national and international attention while retaining its locally led status.

On Friday 12 April 2013, Woodside announced they would not proceed with the planned gas hub at James Price Point. They claimed it was an economic decision and nothing to do with protestors. We beg to differ. Our actions left Woodside shareholders and joint venture partners in no doubt that the company did not have a social licence to build their plant near our town. The company's final investment decision (FID) was set back by over a year due to delays in scheduled testing work caused by our protest activity. In that time the cost of developing the site rose sharply while the global gas market was flooded with cheap gas from the USA, thereby making the project unviable.

Although Woodside has decided on an alternative option – processing the gas off- shore – the threat to life in Broome has not totally disappeared, as the WA government now wants to turn the project site into a supply base for off-shore gas projects. However, our resolve is strong and the energy and skills that helped our community defeat a goliath-sized opponent intact.

The threat of a project in our backyard was a great motivator. And most of us would say that being part of the campaign has left our lives richer and our community stronger. We've made lifelong friends with people we would not otherwise have met, had experiences not previously part of our daily lives, and shared more laughs than tears. It doesn't get better than that.

Fiona Dean

When talk of the proposed gas plant at James Price Point was still a whisper, my sister in Melbourne emailed me with a petition against the project. It stated the gas plant would be 400 kilometres from Broome. I was shocked that the project was being seriously considered and had already progressed to petition stage; and I was upset that people were getting the wrong information. They did not know that JPP was actually just 40 kilometres from our town. I wrote to the petitioners telling them of their error, and my interest and commitment against the gas project snowballed. I sought out any information I could find on the project, determined to share it with as many people as possible. In my little shop I told customers who showed the slightest interest about the project. I was more interested in educating them than selling clothes; I needed to make them aware of what was happening to our beloved Kimberley.

Daryl and I followed the ongoing blockade at Manari corner that was stopping equipment reaching the project site. We celebrated their success at holding up progress of Woodside's vandals. Then, on the 30th night of the blockade, we heard a 'call to arms' for Broome locals to head out to the site. Premier Barnett had ordered police to break through the blockade. I told Daryl, 'It's now or never.' We joined the other protestors there that Tuesday morning. I was traumatised by the violence of the events that day, which became known in Broome as 'Black Tuesday', and felt utterly betrayed by our government and the riot squad that was protecting big business at our expense. This is our home!

After that awful day I was even more determined to spread the word to all who would listen. I compiled No Gas info packs, which contained articles on all aspects of the project. As the existence of these info packs became known, requests came to supply them to campaign information stalls, school projects and interstate festivals, to name just a few. I spent every spare minute on researching, editing, printing and distributing.

Daryl Dean

Since Woodside's announcement to withdraw from the James Price Point option, I have been asked many times why I fought so hard for the campaign against the gas and, of course, there are so many reasons. But mostly I remember the pain and disgust I felt after the shocking events of 'Black Tuesday', when I was rugby-tackled face first into the dirt by two cops after I ran in front of the truck carrying a bulldozer, stopping it for a brief moment on its trip to JPP to desecrate the country there.

Afterward I nursed my cracked ribs, wrenched shoulder and grazed elbow while drowning my shock and indignation with many beers, and I came to the frightening realisation of what a momentous fight lay ahead. I went outside late that night, grabbed a can of spray paint and defiantly graffitied my own work ute with NO GAS, in letters half a metre high, along both sides. From then on, I was totally committed to telling everyone in Broome about the impending disaster the gas project would be to our home.

We adorned our home with No Gas signs. James, our permanently protesting, placard-carrying dummy tied to our front fence, was a hit with the neighbours and many stopped by to chat about and get the latest news on the protest's progress. We found a new talent in dummy making, thinking up slogans and making signs, placards and flags for protest actions. We joined others protesting at actions whenever we could. We met with the Broome Community NO GAS Campaign, joining with others to help make decisions and organise events – none of which we had done before.

We've learned new skills and made so many new and wonderful friends, all united in our commitment to the cause.

Ali Batten

The threat crept up on some of us to begin with. It hovered like an ugly little shadow in the background. How naive we were.

Would we have done as we did if we'd known how many years there were ahead of us? Standing on hot dust-clogged roads in front of vehicles; writing submissions; challenging all levels of government; sleeping in the bush knowing we might be woken at any minute to join the blockade; confronting ignorance and aggression and violence; constructing communications centres in the bush and keeping them maintained and attended; surveying 60 kilometres of roads and an entire town-site at all hours; giving information to people at stalls and rallies and street corners; attending endless meetings and workshops; spending nights in the lock up, days in court, days and nights with our arms locked into metal tubes or around machinery in the middle of the road as we watched convoys of drill rigs and paddy wagons bear down on us; hauling water and firewood, food and camp supplies; repairing broken down vehicles; facing squadrons of riot police intent on destroying us; spending every waking hour on blue to red alert; inventing means of raising funds for everything from court costs and lock-on equipment, rallies and concerts, right down to mosquito masks for blockaders.

Yes, we would have. And we'll be doing all this again if need be. The magical times, the many times of immense beauty, the creativity and the strength we found within ourselves and as a community made the rest of it bearable, and so very worthwhile.

Lahea Levi

I limited my children's exposure to the Gas Hub issue, yet one day my son asked what would happen to the hermit crabs that live at James Price Point. Like it or not, to an eight-year-old boy, hermit crabs are a very important issue, especially as he has spent countless hours on camping trips making friends with these crabs. 'The whales are big enough to get away; the hermit crabs will just get squashed,' he said. I realised he was crying.

I started reconsidering whether as adults we prioritise issues correctly. I started thinking of all the intricate ecosystems, our limited understanding of the microscopic worlds and what we are willing to compromise for the economy. There is no logic in these sorts of decisions.

Joining a campaign to protect the Kimberley was reassuring for me and my family. It gave us hope. Here was a community standing up for the simple necessities and rights of clean air, water and environment; appreciating what is so often taken for granted; defending our lifestyle; supporting what supports us.

I guess abundance, prosperity and wealth are measured and gained differently by different people. Here in the Kimberley we already have all of these things. We hold one of the world's last remaining wildernesses. This needs to be remembered when we plan for its future.

Preserving the Kimberley is not our choice. It is our duty and responsibility to the world and future generations.

Fiona Dean

It will take a very long time to heal the hurt that Broome has suffered as a community. After living here for nearly 30 years, we have many friends and acquaintances. Premier Barnett's attempt to impose this project on our town has caused such a huge rift between some of us.

I am worried there will always be an unresolved gap between the anti-gassers and the pro-gassers due to our fundamental differences in awareness and consciousness. I worry about what the future holds for Broome and the Kimberley. Our 'normal' lives changed for the better by being involved with this campaign and I feel we are now forever fully committed to saving the Kimberley.

◇◇

JAN LEWIS *has spent 20 of the last 30 years in the Kimberley. She thought she'd retired from activism (in the anti-nuclear/social justice movements) and was content to watch birds in the bush, but the potential for the gas hub port to open up the region to mining was enough to recall her to the frontline. She felt great standing strong alongside traditional owners and such dedicated, smart protectors.*

◇◇

FIONA and DARYL DEAN *have been Broome residents since 1985 and are the owners of two small businesses in town. Fiona's only previous involvement in protest action was against the Vietnam War in her schooldays; Daryl had never protested about anything before – so this was a life changer for both. They are now politically awake and have lost all confidence in, and feel betrayed by, the two major political parties.*

◇◇

ALI BATTEN *is one of the 'lock-on grannies', as dubbed by the media. In fact, she is a woman with grandkids who call her Ali and are delighted to have a grandmother who is an environmental activist, standing up for the future of the planet they inherit. She believes this is our greatest challenge and responsibility. Her other role is as an artist.*

◇◇

LAHEA LEVI *has two children. Whenever she and her children can, they spend time in the bush working with her mother and partner on landcare and harvesting native plants for their business. Gubinge* (Terminalia ferdinandiana) *is their main product, one of the richest sources of vitamin C known. They all believed that the air pollution from the gas plant would destroy this enterprise.*

Remembering the Women's Camp at Pine Gap, 1983

BIFF WARD

The phone call came at 1.00 am. I had been asleep all of half an hour. My feet hit the vinyl floor of my Alice Springs bedroom and took me to the phone in three seconds. The events of the day meant I'd only been half asleep anyway.

Sunday 13 November 1983 was the day 111 women had been arrested for trespassing on Commonwealth property at Pine Gap, the US spy base near Alice Springs. These 111 women fostered an image noteworthy in its own right, but when all but a few declared their name to be Karen Silkwood, they became the 'Karen Silkwood 111'. The media was captivated.

So how did this clever action come about?

For six months I, along with many others, had worked to prepare the stage for a women's-only camp outside the gates of 'the base' as the children of the American staff called it. My high school daughter was going steady with one of them, so when Soviet Russia shot down a commercial Korean plane in September of that year and the US invaded Grenada in late October, she told me, twice, 'The base is on red alert.' Maybe this would be the day a mushroom cloud would appear over Mt Gillen, blinding us all and covering the town with radioactive ash. I rode to work wondering if I would ever see her again.

We were planning to camp at the gates to the base, fortified by high cyclone fences and guarded by men in dark glasses. Some local women with the requisite knowledge had negotiated, proper way, with the Aboriginal custodians of the land outside the gates and discovered that the right side of the road was men's place and we were not to go there. The left side was a strip of red earth, spinifex and mulga, ten metres wide at the maximum, bounded on one side by a barbed-wire fence and on the other by the bitumen road to the base.

Half-a-dozen women came months early to help arrange the camp infrastructure: toilets, water and a hessian arrangement for showers. They leafleted the town and produced publicity materials for our support groups in the cities. In the end, some 500 women arrived, most in 'affinity groups', women who shared camping gear and operated as a decision-making unit.

The first day was the 11 November. We liked the resonances with Armistice Day, the coup that dismissed the Whitlam government and the hanging of Ned Kelly in 1881, feeling they conferred a sweet gravitas to our camp outside the base. Led by local Aboriginal women, we arrived *en masse* with our placards, a banner two metres high and 100 metres long, a PA system and all our camping gear. After standing in scorching heat for speeches and songs, we set up camp. That day and into the night, women, alone or in groups, wandered up to the gate and leaned, looking in, thinking and murmuring about what we might do.

Next day we tried to make this decision. We were dazed with heat and the exigencies of the day before and we didn't yet know each other's calibre. Someone suggested we withdraw into affinity groups and talk about: How do you feel? What do you want to do? How could you do it?

When we reconvened in the cool of late afternoon, one group

issued invitations to a 'tea party on the lawn' for the next day, the 13 November. It was the anniversary of the death of a heroine, Karen Silkwood, who died in mysterious circumstances in 1974 after exposing malpractice at the nuclear power plant where she worked in Oklahoma. It gave us the focus we needed. Another group offered to create street theatre as a lead-in.

The 'lawn' was a bright green expanse inside the fence in front of the guardhouse. With a combination of street theatre to distract the police and a sudden subtle prearranged shift, hundreds of women breached the gate with a huge push and an axe meeting a cable at just the right moment. We were in. Teapots and cakes arrived, mugs were produced and tea was drunk amid laughter and exclamations of disbelief. Women wandered freely between 'inside' and 'outside' for some hours.

The gigantic circle held a meeting to decide who wanted to go further – to the base over the hill – and how to do it. An encampment of police with paddy wagons and tent infrastructure waited at the top of the hill. I realised that I needed to stay and forgo the adrenalin of getting arrested because, as an Alice Springs woman with contacts, I would probably be needed on the outside.

I drove my car – a battered FJ wagon called Maggie – up to the flattened fence and parked sideways so that as many as possible could stand on the roof and the bonnet to watch – a balcony view. We watched some 150 of us in a bunch, walking very slowly up the road. Later, we heard that the woman who needed to walk with tiny slow steps had been made the leader.

As they neared the crest, the police moved in. Some escaped and ran, hallooing, back to us. But on the hillside, too far away to hear, we watched women being taken behind canvas, police running about, vehicles moving in. It took a long time for us to realise they had taken the arrested women out the back way in paddy wagons and would not be coming through the gates where we waited.

The 111 'Karen Silkwoods' refused bail (with a few exceptions who left the gaol for health reasons), so the camp was a quarter empty that night while the lock-up was full. When I answered that 1.00 am phone call, a woman's voice said, 'Something dreadful is happening. All the women are screaming.'

'I'll be right there,' I said.

I stepped out the back door and heard it, a cacophony of shrieking chaos scything through the night into my dark backyard. It came from the police station, 300 metres from my house as a cockatoo would fly. I thought of the coup in Chile 10 years before; the shrieks in the night.

At the front of the police station, there was a group of our lawyers. They had been granted a little access and knew that because of the Karen Silkwood name game, the police were trying to fingerprint the women – who were not cooperating. It was said someone's thumb had been broken. The noise of the women flowed over and through our conversation, ebbing and flowing but loud, like a storm.

The lawyers said, 'We need information – from the women. See what you can do.'

I had never before taken any notice of the back part of the lock-up. A friend and I walked down the side street: cyclone fence, a line of cells in a concrete block and lots of streetlights. We continued until we could squeeze into a wasteland at the rear where a cellblock came close to the fence.

'Hey,' we called. 'Hey. Who's in there?'

A woman I knew well. Six or more to a cell. They quietened the women nearby and told us who'd been injured, who was ill, what the police were saying and that there was no toilet paper. We reported back to the lawyers who'd been joined by a doctor. More questions. So back and forth we went, spies on the night-time street.

The sky lightened to dove-grey and birds began to warble. We were on another trip from the back to the front when three Aboriginal youths came walking toward us. We veered to go around them but the one in the middle veered too and walked right up to me, saying, 'Thank you, sister, thank you,' in the soft rolling sibilant sound of that country.

'What for?' I asked, truly puzzled.

'Last night,' he said, 'was the first time in my life that the police didn't come to our camp.'

'Oh. Oh my god,' we breathed.

'Yes,' he nodded. 'Thank you.'

'You're welcome.'

This exchange in whispering voices as we stood beside the noisy gaol in the murky light.

That Monday, 14 November 1983, every major newspaper in Australia had a front-page story about the 111 'Karen Silkwoods'. Some of the stories included claims by the police that we had 'repeatedly assured' them that 'no assault would be made on the installation'. We hadn't, of course. Rather, we had repeatedly assured them (a) we would not be violent, and (b) we had no plans for action because all the women would decide what was to happen, after we had gathered together on the 11th. Our slogan was 'Close Pine Gap' but our goal was to raise awareness of the place and its function among the Australian populace. We'd done it! We had accomplished an activist's dream.

Our success was so enormous that we could hardly take it in.

There was the wild night in the gaol, the likes of which the police had not encountered before. We had 111 court cases, which one magistrate heard in a stream of 'personal statements' that moved many, including journalists, to tears. The magistrate acknowledged, over and over, the sincerity of the women's passionate words. We were also besieged by the media and we'd had no sleep.

Then money started flooding in from all over the country. It came from individuals, groups and, surprisingly to us, a bunch of hairy-legged feminists, from many quintessentially masculine groups such as unionised seamen, wharfies and coal miners. We had one woman looking after our pathetic bank balance and, luckily, another woman stepped forward and said, 'I can help with that. I'm a bookkeeper.' A plaited rainbow wristband was immediately tied around her wrist denoting 'Woman Carrying A Special Responsibility'.

The manager of the Alice Springs YWCA had provided their hall and a phone for our headquarters. Unbeknown to us, she did this on her personal recognisance, because the vast majority of her board wanted nothing to do with Those Radical Women.

The phone rang hot. I fielded a call from a Labor senator whom I knew slightly. It was early in the Hawke government and she was screaming at me that we'd set the anti-war movement back decades, that we ought not to be undertaking direct action in this high-handed way, that 'we' – the peace movement – didn't believe in arrestable actions. She was crying. I think I laughed.

'No, Pat, it's fine. This won't set anything back.'

I couldn't begin to describe to her the creative explosion outside the gates that had led to the Karen Silkwoods. Or how we were doing all this with red sand in our food, giant prickles inside our swags and the occasional willy-willy whisking whole writing pads and flannel shirts across the fence into forbidden Commonwealth territory.

While the 111 Karen Silkwoods talked to the magistrate, others painted a huge notice on the road outside the gate: Pine Gap – Opened by (then a women's symbol combined with a peace symbol) to the Public. The gate had been patched up and the women painted on one of the planks used for reinforcement: A Hasty Erection.

The next evening, the Aboriginal women who had led us the first day visited. They wanted to check that anyone crazy enough to actually court arrest was okay. It underscored the gulf: we could use the police system for political purposes while for them it was a frontline agent of the invasion of their country and their lives.

In the aftermath, some women moved to Alice Springs to work in Indigenous organisations. Other women became full-time anti-war activists. Lots discovered feminism in a way they hadn't before. Along dusty roadways that can't be measured, behaviours spread out from that action to become part of the fabric of the nation.

◇◇

BIFF WARD *is a feminist, social activist and writer who was a key member of the Women for Survival anti-nuclear group that operated in the 80s. She wrote* Father-Daughter Rape, *the first Australian book about child sexual abuse in 1984 and was the first Equal Opportunity Officer at the South Australian Institute of Technology. She is now a full-time writer; her memoir,* In My Mother's Hands, *was published in 2014, long-listed for The Stella Prize 2014 and short-listed for the NSW Premier's Non-fiction Prize.*

Acknowledgements

Our thanks go to the people who contributed their stories to this book.

Our thanks also go to Greg Martin who helped with editing, as well acting as a sounding board along the way. We would also like to thank Marjon Martin, Chilla Bulbeck, Fiona Verity and Fiona Johnson for their ideas and input.

Printed in Australia
AUOC01n1546200416
275354AU00002B/2/P